ANCIENT WALLS OF EAST ANGLIA

ANCIENT WALLS OF EAST ANGLIA

by

RENE BECKLEY

TERENCE DALTON LIMITED

LAVENHAM . SUFFOLK

1979

Published by
TERENCE DALTON LIMITED
ISBN 0 900963 93 X

*Illustrations, maps and photographs are by the author,
unless otherwise stated*

Text photoset in 11/12pt. Baskerville

Printed in Great Britain at
THE LAVENHAM PRESS LIMITED
LAVENHAM   .   SUFFOLK

© Rene Beckley 1979

Contents

Index of Illustrations

Introduction and Acknowledgement

WALL, an evocative word, conjures up myriad images. The walls of our houses, with all their emotive connotations of life. Most of us have heard about the walls of the Lascaux Caves; Angkor Wat; the terrace walls of Sacsayhuaman; Jericho, Persepolis and Babylon; and the Great Wall of China which can be seen from the moon. Everywhere walls.

This book came into being because I accidentally discovered some superb engravings of medieval city gates. This led to a searching out of the sites of these gates and the remains of the walls they once served. The quest then grew to encompass the whole of East Anglia, in terms of walled defences.

Early man took over behind trees and rocks, a passive defence. When pre-historic man raised his arm to protect himself against foe or marauding animal, he was using the first form of shield, so that his defence became active. From the rock and the raised arm came the ideas by which villages, towns and cities clothed themselves in defensive banks, ditches and walls. They used slings, stones, arrows and spears, swords, ballistae, cannons and other engines of war — in conjunction with the story of the walls.

To all the people who helped — my most grateful thanks: to Libraries, Record Offices and Museums all over East Anglia; to the Ministry of Defence; the Department of Environment; to Estate Publications; The Harwich Society; The Lord Chamberlain's Office; The Property Services Agency and to Mrs M. P. Harper, Photographic Librarian in particular; to Dr J. Alexander, Stuart R. Bacon, Fletcher & Son Ltd., Norwich, Mr E. C. Kerry and Councillor L. T. Weaver.

Not least of all my thanks to — Mr P. Hepworth, one-time City Librarian of Norwich, for his generous help and permission to use Local Studies materials; Mrs Irene Read for helping with research at Bedford, Tempsford and Hertford; and Miss Gladys Read. Finally to Miss Dorothy Kendall who helped with typing and who travelled many of the four thousand miles with me in my research.

Rene Beckley
Keswick, Norwich,
Norfolk.
May, 1979

Dedicated to Dorothy Kendall

St Martins Gate, Norwich, by John Crome

Norwich Castle Museum

viii

1. By Stane Street

WITHAM — PLESHEY — HERTFORD

Witham

EAST Anglia is a vast network of rivers and remains of former Roman roads. When the Romans conquered Britain it was largely via East Anglia that they reached the rest of Britain. They constructed a tracery of straight highways over the land, as far north as the Firth of Forth where they built the Antonine Wall, which stretched across to the Firth of Clyde. Many of these thoroughfares roughly followed the course of already existing ancient British trackways.

The main Roman east-west road of southern East Anglia was reached by a minor spur road from the great Balkerne Gate at Colchester. This major road, Stane Street, carved its way across country through Braintree, Great Dunmow and Bishop's Stortford to the road centre at Braughing on Ermine Street, that most remembered of all British Roman roads. A few miles south of Stane Street, Witham, Pleshey and Hertford lie in a line east to west, the latter actually on the Roman road, and indeed on the more important prehistoric early British trackway, the Icknield Way. This ancient way led from Wiltshire to a point just east of Hunstanton on the Wash.

Witham stands only one and a half miles from another Roman road, the Great Road, which led from London to Colchester. The many Roman finds in the area prove without doubt the existence of a nearby Roman settlement. Such highways as the Romans built must have had profound effect on the towns and villages nearby.

Witham had a multivallate hillfort, built in the bend of the River Brain. Such hillfort walls were thrown up with the ramparts some distance apart. Ditches were dug and the topsoil put aside and the ramparts were made of the heavier soil from underneath. Various Iron Age materials have been found in the environs of Witham as well as traces of ancient burials and a silver St Edmund penny.

1

Witham Mound was originally an Iron Age fort erected, according to some authorities, subsequent to 1000 B.C. British tin coins of the first century B.C., a bone comb and a loom weight are among the Witham finds, as well as Iron Age pottery. The town had access to the sea via the River Blackwater, so was undoubtedly settled at an early date.

The Trinovantes, a Celtic tribe, lived in the area where, shortly before the birth of Christ, they were subjugated by Cunobelin (Shakespeare's Cymbeline) the warrior king of the Belgae.

Many burhs or stockaded strongholds* were built by Edward the Elder, the son of King Alfred, to defend Saxon lands against Danish invaders. These new burhs were usually made near an existing settlement. Therefore it may be assumed that the burh at Witham came into being after an original settlement.

In 912 King Edward went with his forces to Maldon in Essex and camped there while the burh was being made and constructed at Witham. And in 913, "in the summer between gang-days (Rogation days), and mid summer, went King Edward with some of his forces into Essex, and encamped there the while that (his) men worked and built the burh at witham." "Edward worht and getimbrede aet Witham." The former outer rampart surrounded some twenty-six acres, while the inner rampart enclosed about ten acres, with a fortress inside. The fort is not thought to have survived after 940 A.D.

This burh, probably built by the king, is the mound near Witham Station. Extensive damage was done to the mound in 1843 when the railway line was cut through its centre, but this may have saved the whole being levelled later for housing purposes. Despite its partial destruction, the mound, it is still claimed, is one of the two best remaining examples of a Saxon burh and further archaeological knowledge may come from that which remains.

During Edward the Confessor's reign Witham had one manor, 21 villeins, six serfs, 18 ploughs and 30 acres of meadow. The town at the time of Domesday was of obvious importance because of the number of entries in the Book. Edward most probably built that part of the town situated on Chipping Hill, round the church, which stands about half a mile north-west from the other part of the town. Here are considerable remains of a circular camp, defended by double vallum, almost levelled within on the south-west where the road from hence to Braintree runs along the outer bank; the river defending it on the west side and there the works are lower; a road runs through it from north to south.

"Nowadays little thought is given to this burh. Motorists when emerging from the Avenue and Avenue Road fail to realise that the steep slope they have to negotiate is the relic of the defensive bank of the ancient fortification. In former years it was a well-known landmark and was mentioned by most writers who included Witham in their histories," says M. L. Smith in his *Early History*

*Burh later became burgh and borough.

The Mound at Witham cut in half by the railway with factories built on its slopes.

of Witham. The exciting thing about places like Witham is that they demand so much of the imagination to fill in long vanished details. Chipping Hill by the river is a quiet scene where indeed fancy may run riot; where, away from the clamorous din of trains and cars one may "listen" for the tramp of Roman legions, or the chipping sound of Iron Age tools.

The mound is singularly uninteresting today, with its massive dissection. However it deserves more than a passing thought when one remembers that Witham Mound stood supreme for nine hundred years before the railway scalpel performed its surgery, and for how many hundreds of years before that back into Iron Age days? Will any vestige of the mound remain nine hundred years hence? What did the mound mean to Iron Age people? Shall we ever know?

*　　*　　*　　*　　*

Pleshey

A stone inscribed RICARDVS REX II is set up in Pleshey Church. No doubt the tablet once took pride of place at Pleshey castle, for King Richard II would ensure that all knew to whom the castle belonged.

The Normans are said to have given Pleshey its name. Some say Pleshey or Plaisy, a corruption of the French plaisir — pleasure, or otherwise agreeable prospect. Pleshey in the twentieth century is indeed most pleasant. However, Plaisseis or Plaieseiz also signifies an enclosure, a much more likely meaning referring to the rampart and ditch surrounding the village. The Saxons named it Tumblestoun, meaning tumuli or hills.

3

The earthworks are believed to have been raised by the Saxons or Danes. But Plesheybury is marked on the Ordnance Survey Iron Age map as having ancient burials. Pleshey is certainly among the oldest villages in England. P. A. Rahtz, in his 1960 interim report on Pleshey, says it is possible that the present enormous earthworks were thrown up shortly before 1180 because a great grandson of the original Geoffrey de Mandeville was given permission to fortify, or perhaps re-fortify, his castle at Pleshey.

If Plesheybury was settled however in the Iron Age period, and H.M.Ordnance Survey maps are not usually wrong, how then could the Normans have given it its name in the eleventh century? They must merely have re-affirmed the name of an ancient site. Bury means to enclose, which would suggest that the village in the Iron Age period was enclosed, and thus defended, if only from marauding animals. Was there a man-made "hill" at Plesheybury then and later did the Normans merely top it up? Certainly the Saxon name of Tumblestoun would seem to confirm an early mound. Plesheybury lay on a tributary of the Chelmer, which in turn was a tributary of the River Blackwater.

The village once had a large Roman farmstead or perhaps in those times it was but a small village settlement, as yet archaeologists are uncertain. What is certain is that many Roman finds have been unearthed west of the church — stone coffins, glass urns with bones, Roman mosaics, pieces of iron, human bones and bronze vessels of the first century A.D. The church at Pleshey is partly built with Roman tiles. Part of the Roman entrenchment was probably destroyed when the castle and great mound were erected. The perimeter of the vallum is almost one Roman mile*, while the earthworks have an area of some two acres, enclosed by strong, high embankments, deep moated on the outside. To the east is an immense mound called the Mount, which is separated from the enclosed area and the surrounding grounds by a deep ditch. This mound is called the Keep and at one time had a Norman castle built on its summit. It was a terraced motte and bailey with traces of a second bailey, making a figure eight plan, inset into a carotid village enclosure.

In 1800 four Roman roads which led into the entrenchment were easily traced and many Roman remains have been found in the surrounding areas. Certainly Pleshey is no distance from the main north-west Roman road from Chelmsford to Great Chesterford. The earthworks cover some 11½ acres on a spur near the confluence of two streams. The moats were water-filled and probably drained by a system of controls. One part of the moat near the modern entrance to the castle is still full of water.

Many villages crowded beside their castle to gain protection. But sometimes the village was enclosed inside a bank and ditch running from the castle bailey, thus forming a defensive whole. Pleshey is just such a village. An

*Roman mile was 1,000 paces.

The present village of Pleshey lies inside the Town Enclosure with the church just outside to centre right of picture.   *Southend Air Photography Limited*

oval mount rises from the bailey ditch to the west. At one time there would have been a central "platform"for a double wooden bridge, most likely a drawbridge. This would give access from the Town Enclosure and Bailey across the dry part of the moat to the platform, carried on piles over the water-filled moat and up a sloping bridge to the timber keep. The motte, or flat-topped mound, of the early Norman castle, was a very old form of defence. This once supported an earth and timber stockade with a wooden tower inside. A keep—stone tower—was built on the motte at a later date, the foundations of which are thought to be still there under the mound.

"There is a Castell hill, and banks, and motes," said a land agent in 1641 in the mention of this old castle, the "seyte of the Honor of Mandeville", soon after the Conquest, "and which was two or three hundred years since the mansion house of great dukes and peeres of this realm, out of which castle the duke of Glocester, uncle to King Richard the 2nd., was suddenly taken and carryed over to Callis and there murdered." So Pleshey has a history.

Pleshey castle's history is largely the history of the life of the inhabitants of this defended village. The inhabitants must have helped to build the castle; throw up the ramparts; dig and clean the moat; build the drawbridge; and surround the village with the Town Enclosure. Although this book is not strictly about castles, Pleshey, like Framlingham in Suffolk, must be mentioned because the village was enclosed with walls and the villagers must indeed have helped to people the armies of its castle's owners.

The ownership of the village of Pleshey changed hands repeatedly in former times. Originally William the Conqueror made a gift of it to Eustace, Count of Bologne. The Count's son later inherited, as did his granddaughter Maud in her turn. Then it passed to King Stephen, through his marriage to the Count's daughter, Matilda. Stephen later gave it to Geoffrey de Mandeville, who started the building of his castle there in 1140, although what form the castle took at that time is not known.

When Geoffrey de Mandeville led his first crusade he conquered Jerusalem and was offered the kingship but refused because "he would not wear a crown of gold where his Saviour wore a crown of thorns." When de Mandeville rebelled against the king by joining forces with the king's cousin and rival, the Empress Matilda, troops poured into the enclosed village and seized the Earl who was then imprisoned in the Tower of London. This act was a quirk of fate because the Earl was himself Constable of the Tower of London. His castles at Walden and the uncompleted castle at Pleshey were demanded by the king as the price of his release. The destruction of these two castles was ordered in 1157-8. However the estates were later restored to the dead earl's son, Geoffrey. When the second de Mandeville died in 1167, the castle of Pleshey passed to his brother William. After William's death, his son, also William, saw to the completion of the castle.

A superb ancient brick bridge spans the moat to the old Pleshey Mount.

The people of Pleshey involved with the comings and goings of troops must have lived under threat of destruction and devastation after the surrender of the castle. An inventory made for King Richard II, after he seized the castle at Pleshey, belonging to his uncle, the Duke of Gloucester, showed in one item alone the luxury in which Pleshey's powerful owners lived. The Duke's bed has been described as, "a great bed of gold, that is to say, a coverlet, a tester, and the entire celure of fine blue satin wrought with garters of gold, and three curtains tartaryn beaten to match. Also two long and four square pillows of the set of the bed." But for all his riches the Duke was a lost man, for having married the heiress of Pleshey, becoming its lord, he plotted against the king. A betrayal took place and the king came to Pleshey to ask his uncle to attend a council in London. Enroute Gloucester was seized by the Earl of Nottingham, and taken to Calais where he was murdered by suffocation between two feather beds.

The present village, with blacksmith's shop and flower-decked cottages, lies inside the Town Enclosure. To the north there is a brook and water-filled ditch and some remaining ramparts. Only the church and some nearby buildings lie outside this defensive system. Much of the perimeter earthwork extends well beyond the limit of the twentieth century village of Pleshey.

It is difficult for the uninitiated to define the lay-out of this set of earthworks, they are so enormous. But with the aid of a map and the current guide to the castle, given a sunny day and an urge to walk, one may well join the men of Pleshey—long ago. It is difficult even from the top of the mount to make out what lies within the Town Enclosure, for in summer the trees hide the view of the village. However even in a summer season with trees all around, one has a clear view for over 20 miles in all directions around Essex. The mound is reminiscent of Thetford and Silbury.

Pleshey castle is now a place of grazing sheep and thistles, of ducks drifting on the moat, and a superb ancient brick bridge, spanning the moat to the old mound.

*   *   *   *   *

Hertford

A visit to Hertford Museum jolts one back into pre-history. Here in glass show cases lie Mammouth bones, a Mammouth tusk, the tusk of a Woolly Rhinoceros, a Hippopotamus tooth; all found at Water Hall Farm, at Hertingfordbury, a mere two miles out of town. By the farm a copse of shimmering silver-green trees with leaves twisting and turning in a strong wind has a strange air of the primeval. Stone hand-axes, Pleistocene forms of antlers, shark bones, reptile paddle bones, sea urchins, shells similar to oysters, crocodile bones, ammonites, reptile teeth, sponges, along with finds of

Roman pottery from nearby areas, point not only to early times but to pre-history.

The grounds of Hertford castle are reached via two wooden footbridges, from a central car park. These bridges cross the rivers Lee and Lea where they join beside the old Norman motte, or mound. The flat-topped mound, some 15-16 feet high, is largely hidden behind trees. On its summit one might be standing on top of an elephant's foot and it seems hardly any larger being small as mounds go. The view from the summit shows river, swans, castle, town buildings, all somewhat obstructed by small trees. This is the motte of motte and bailey earthwork, the earliest part of what remains of Hertford's defences. Originally this was part of a Norman castle consisting of a fortified mound surrounded by an earthen bank and ditch.

Hertford castle is known to have been fully provisioned in 1173, so the building itself must have been completed and the castle bridge had to be repaired in 1182 at the cost of one pound. Pipe Rolls tell of expenditure on works in the castle in 1191, under Richard I, when John landed in England and a threat of French invasion was imminent. An allowance for 10 knights and 20 men at arms with two horses was made at that time, as well as 20 footmen, and the castle was garrisoned with royal troops. The castle was beseiged by Lewis of France in 1216, but held out for 24 days. Queen Isabella, mother of Edward III, had the castle and town of Hertford for life in 1327, but lost it three years later, when Mortimer, with whom she controlled the country, was seized and put to death, to regain it once more a year later from her son. The castle, near London as it was, kept her within easy sight of her son should she again intrigue against his crown.

Queen Elizabeth I's charter to Hertford gave also a Common Seal, a hart standing in a ford forming a rebus on the name of the town, between its antlers a long cross "patee fitchee". On the further bank of the right hand a tripple towered castle, each tower domed, embattled, and topped with a cross, portcullis half down in the round-headed doorway, on the left a tree.

By 1610 most of the castle buildings had been pulled down and only "one fair Gate-house of brick, one tower of brick, and the old walls of the said Castle," remained.

In 1700 Chauncy spoke of the rivers of Hertford, "through which the Rivers Lea, Mimeram and Benifician pass, to make this Town delightful to the inhabitants." It is still a delight today. The last two charming names have vanished into time leaving only the unromantic Beane crossing the north-west corner of the town. However the Lea and the Lee, when seen laid out on a map, romantically seem to tie a lover's knot in the centre, with ribbons of water streaming out on either side.

There were two tenth century Saxon burhs in Hertford — both would have been defended. To quote A. G. Davies, Curator of Hertford Museum: "It

The second wooden bridge leading to Hertford Castle Mound which lies behind the trees to the left.

would however be misleading to suggest that their course is certain at any point, as no trace of them survived to be recorded on the earliest maps of the town, a recent excavation produced no unequivocal evidence of the line."

About 913 Edward the Elder, during his campaign against the Danes, established a burh between the rivers Maram (Mimram), Beane and Lea. This burh on the north, and the rivers guarding the other three sides, is said to have been an effective and important defence. Mr. Davies said that the "Northern Burh seems to have been a peninsula burh, on a spur of gravel, surrounded by marsh, and is marked by St. Andrew's Street. The Southern Burh line of defence here is drawn to include all those of the ancient streets that seem to fit into a rectilinear pattern, and to exclude features known to have been outside the town, e.g. The Priory. It is presumed that the Norman Castle was built straddling the defences."

When work on the Northern Burh was completed the King went to Maldon to superintend the building of a burh at Witham (Essex). The following year he returned to Hertford and "wrought the burh" on the southern side of the River Lea. One historian describes a palisade of wood as the defence, while another says of Edward, that he "surrounded the whole (area) with a rude wall of turf, and converted it into a borough." Though Hertford had early defences, there remains little record of those earliest times.

The boundary between Danelaw and Saxon England was the River Lee, and the early importance of the town was due to its ford, giving easy access to the north. Hertford was unimportant in Roman times for Ermine Street crossed the Lee further north near Ware, hence the Roman finds in that area, at Much Hadham, Welwyn and Sawbridgeworth. When the Romans left Britain their bridges fell into disuse and the Saxons again reverted to using fords. With the Norman Conquest Ware Bridge was re-built. This caused strife between Hertford and Ware as the former, possessing a castle, imposed its will on Ware. The Hertford authorities went so far as to close Ware Bridge to vehicles, by the use of chains, during the thirteenth century.

A thriving community existed long before the arrival of the Romans and as the capital of the East Saxons it was called Heorotford. When King John captured the Black Prince, he was brought to Hertford castle in 1359. No distance away Edmund Tudor, the father of the first Tudor monarch, Henry VII, was born at Much Hadham and nearer still, at Hatfield Palace, Elizabeth I was in residence when she received news of her accession to the throne. So the town has not been unacquainted with greatness and important people. In fact it housed the Court and Parliament on more than one occasion when it became the Palace of Hertford Castle, the Courts being temporarily moved from Westminster in 1582 and 1592-3, when the plague overtook London.

Today Hertford castle is a red brick building decorated with crenellations; the Royal Arms of Edward IV; tired and worn stone lions; the building so much restored and rebuilt as to have lost, it seems, much of its appeal to the visual senses. This building is the gatehouse built for Edward IV, altered and

The Northern Burh seems to have been a peninsula burh, surrounded by marsh; the Southern Burh is thought to have been straddled by the Norman castle.

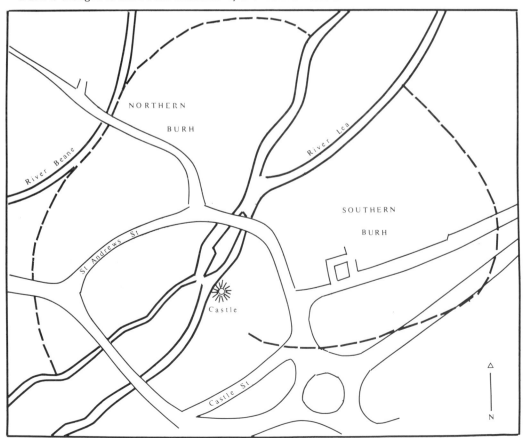

added to one hundred and ninety years ago by the second Marquis of Downshire. The gatehouse turrets still stand and before it, in former days, a drawbridge crossed the moat. The castle has also served as a hunting lodge; a nursery; a prison; a college; a private house and now Council Offices during its almost ten centuries of occupancy.

The lawn in front of the garden side of the castle once housed lodgings of the Court and royal apartments, all timber framed, but no trace of these remains.

The twelfth century curtain wall runs due east from the mound, which the defences originally straddled. Further along the wall is pierced by a gap on either side of which are two high, though slim, eighteenth century round towers, with the original hooks still in the sides, where the castle gates hung.

Where this "gateway" stands a great angle bastion guarded the turn of the castle wall. This has long since gone and a new community activities centre is just outside the wall. Where the two eighteenth century towers stand a former guardhouse protected this back gate to the castle. The towers themselves were guarded by a drawbridge over the inner moat. This draw-bridge led to a barbican across the end of the outer bailey. A second drawbridge kept the outer moat with a further guardhouse, so that there were at that point five separate defences. From here the curtain wall turns south-east, a huge section remaining to a height of about 20 feet. A plaque records that Henry II built the curtain wall, 1170-1171, and here the wall is much repaired flint, with brick at the bottom. Further along the wall is unadulterated flint, then a third section of modern red brick has been inserted where the wall has fallen. Next an arch breaks its way through the wall, but the arch is blocked up by a wooden gate. Here crenellations have been built on the top, and cotoneaster falls from the walls in bright orange bursts. Outside the wall is repaired with brick and imitation crenellations of flint. Inside it is easy to see how the earth was heaped up to the bottom of the wall. Outside the rampart slope is steeper still. It is at this part of the wall, by the arch, that the Southern Burh Wall of 913 curved in to meet the river by the old mound.

Next the wall turns south-west to end in a postern gate and polygonal tower of fourteenth century date. The gate is well repaired and crenellated, with a pointed arch in the centre, and an iron grille gate standing half open. Beside it to the west stands the bastion tower which guarded this foot gate into the castle. Arrow slits are still visible and inside, behind the crenellated top, is a wall walk, which now slopes inwards at such an angle as to make walking a hazard. A ledge running round the tower wall just below the walk reminds us that the tower was roofed.

Immediately outside the gate and following the line of the curtain wall a garden is laid out in the remains of the moat. This is the only part of the former moat to be free of buildings, the remainder being built on when

Charles I gave the castle to the Earl of Salisbury. In the moat a few hundred yards from the postern gate is the remains of an eighteenth century ice pit.

The postern also had a drawbridge outside across the inner moat, protected by the octagonal tower. At the far side of the outer bailey once stood a square guardhouse with four turrets at the corners, and an outer drawbridge. The narrow space between the inner and outer bailey was to the east and south defended by a wooden palisade. The wall from the postern tower was destroyed by gunpowder in the eighteenth century, and the wall which once protected the section from the main gate to the keep alongside the river is now completely gone.

The main gatehouse with its portcullis at the south-west furthermost point of the walling, and another gatehouse, led from the inner bailey to a drawbridge. Plans of Hertford castle do not show a direct entrance opposite this drawbridge from the outer bailey and outer moat.

Defended no longer by its castle Hertford, today, stands by the quiet waters of the River Lea and prepares other defences against the ravages of mechanical vehicles that seem to grow for ever larger.

The inside of the postern gate with a polygonal tower of the fourteenth century at Hertford.

2. Enigmatic Web

CAMBRIDGE — GODMANCHESTER — GREAT CHESTERFORD — BEDFORD — TEMPSFORD

Cambridge

PALEOLITHIC handaxes found in gravel on the Huntingdon Road, chipped pear-shaped stone axes originating a million years ago, testify to the antiquity of Cambridge. Mesolithic tool-kits, small flint chips, set into wooden handles, used as arrow heads, knives and scrapers of the first hunters and gatherers, have been unearthed in the Trumpington area. Neolithic polished stone axes, of the first farmers of Cambridge, were discovered near Newnham and Bronze Age finds, such as socketed chisels, have been discovered in Cambridge. There were Iron Age settlements in the area and a ring-ditch of that period revealed the charred and mutilated skeletons of some mass disaster. Was this ring-ditch the first defensive "wall" of Cambridge?

Many other Iron Age discoveries have been made in or near Cambridge: cemeteries; burials; chariot burials; farms and open settlements all show the area to be occupied in antiquity. A Belgic (first century B.C.) settlement in the area between Mount Pleasant and Castle Street has been definitely established. Excavations in 1972-3 revealed a series of horse-shoe ditches. Finds in these ditches prove the settlers to be Belgae settlers of the Catuvellaunian tribe. After the Roman conquest the enclosure ditch near Castle Street had a new Roman road built over it.

According to the Antonine Itinerary, named after M. Aurelius Antoninus, better known as Caracalla, Cambridge was called Durolipons*. On the Roman map of Britain Durolipons stands on a Roman road between Ermine Street to the west, and the Icknield Way to the east. The Via Devana and Akeman Street are also marked as running through the city. Cambridge — at the centre of a veritable web of Roman roads.

A question mark however still stands beside the Roman name for Cambridge in archaeological books and records.

---

*Royal Commision on Historic Monuments i, lxv-vi states that in later fourth century town thought to have been Durolipons. Text to Map of Roman Britain shows Durolipons followed by question mark which disappears on the map. All thus follow Antonine Itinerary.

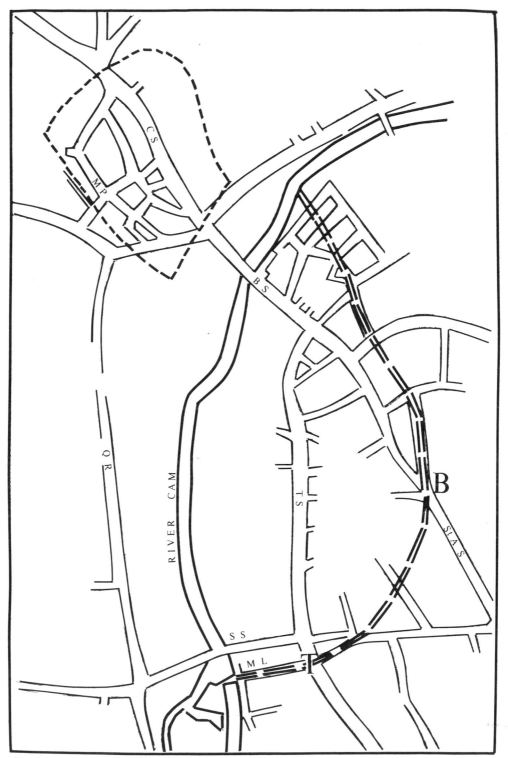

Sketch map with approximate outline of the Roman Town; the line of the King's Ditch;
B-Barnwell Gate, T-Trumpington Gate; BS-Bridge Street, CS-Castle Street, ML-Mill Lane,
MP-Mount Pleasant, QR-Queen's Road, SS-Silver Street, StAS-St Andrew's Street, TS-Trump-
ington Street.

When the Romans settled on a hill overlooking the river in Cambridge during the period 43-70 A.D., they built an enclosure using palisade and ditches as defence. Evidence of this was discovered in 1972. Both parts of the defence were renewed in the first century A.D. During the period circa 70-150 A.D., "a new rectangular enclosure was laid out", enlarging the enclosed area. This "may well have been part of the settlement of the region after the Boudiccan revolt and have been, besides a staging post, an administrative centre connected with the trade of the Car Dyke and the settlement of the fens."* When the ditch was partially excavated it was proved beyond doubt that no wall foundations were ever dug. "The purpose of the enclosure is uncertain. It is unlike normal military works and was probably for official buildings of some sort." The enclosure became a civil settlement in the second century A.D.

During the fourth century some 21 acres of the settlement were enclosed by bank, stone wall, and ditch, with gates, and a town flourished inside. The walls were built by Laeti, German mercenaries who were brought in to defend the town by the Imperial governor. Three Roman Gates are known to have existed and the ruins of the West Gate have been found by archaeologists. The North Gate is said to have been under or near a garage on the Huntingdon Road. The East Gate site is not known, but it would be logical to expect that such a gate was built, as the Romans usually sited their main gates at the cardinal points of the compass, and that it would have been placed opposite the West Gate. The South Gate site has been definitely established, the direct road from the south having been known for a very long time.

The West Gate was found at the junction of Albion Row and Mount Pleasant placed near the middle of the west wall. A rectangular footing, 25 feet by 15 feet, was found at the northern half of the gate. It was impossible to excavate the southern half of the gate, but it was probably located under the pavement of Albion Row. A twenty-eight foot roadway between the two existed and Dr Alexander suggests that the gate had a bastion or tower on either side.

Usually Roman walls were strengthened with bastions, but no trace of these has been found in Cambridge although they probably existed. They may possibly be masked by the medieval castle towers, the motte and the postern and the south east tower, and by the Civil War artillery bastion.

One historian says the Roman Camp of Camboritum, established where a British settlement had stood on the banks of the Roman Granta, eventually became Grantacaester, Grantebrigge, Cantabrigge and finally Cambridge. Through the city the river is the Cam and a tributary, the Granta, runs to Linton. When Rome ceased to rule the township fell into decay and appears to have been deserted from about 400 to 800 A.D, but Roman roads were left radiating out from the town and no one knows what caused the end of the Roman town. Bede says that the monks of Ely went in the year 695 to search

*Dr John Alexander.

The southern end of Cambridge King's Ditch ran from the mill pool at the bottom of Mill Lane.

for a coffin for St Etheldreda, and found a stone sarcophagus near the walls of the little deserted city (*civitalulam quandam desolatum*) called Grantacaestir.

Documents refer to Danish and late Saxon settlement in the area sometime between c.875-1068, but evidence is scanty. During the Saxon period however most of the populace went to live south of the river.

Although there is little evidence of the Saxon period in Cambridge, a ring of Saxon cemeteries around the city does indicate that a Saxon town once lay within the ring. When the Saxons built their bridge across the Granta before 875, the town was called Grantabrycg. Probably this bridge was built during the reign of Offa the Great (757-96), King of Mercia and remote descendant of the founder of the Royal House of East Anglia, a gifted, ambitious man whose aim was to keep the trade outlet to the sea open.

After the Norman Conquest, in 1068, a royal castle was built within the confines of the old Roman settlement area, on the bluff above the river. At this time the western approaches to the castle were cleared, demolishing much that was left of Roman traces. The early castle was a motte and bailey of earth and wood, being later rebuilt of stone. The gatehouse survived until the nineteenth century, although the castle itself was destroyed in 1660.

During the reign of Henry I, the King granted the townspeople a monopoly of the river-borne traffic throughout the county. The town received benefit by trade with five counties and lords of the manor and religious houses turned waste into productive land to gain benefit from the additional trade, even though the tolls belonged to the king. So Cambridge prospered and became rich. But later Cambridge suffered by being sacked in the days of Stephen's reign and the county suffered greatly too. Yet the citizens built no walls or similar defences at that time.

Long before the period however, a ditch was constructed, carving a semi-circular scar across Cambridge. It is not known when the ditch was constructed, although some historians say it was dug for Edward the Elder (899-925) some time after 921. Whether it was a customs barrier or built as a defence is not properly known. However a survey of 1629 calls it the military defence of the town to the south and east of the river, the river being the defence to the west. The Danes could have been said to have "built" it as part of a protective harbour, but they are not known to have been at that point near the river. In some parts of the circuit of the ditch, there was a foot pathway alongside it. As Edward built a similar burh at Bedford on the south loop of the river, it is quite possible he did the same at Cambridge. This ditch was not wide enough to have been of much defensive use except as protection against casual marauders.

This ditch swept in a southern loop from Mill Lane, flowing back into the Cam near Jesus College. Historians state that Cambridge became an important Danish burh, with jurisdiction over a region, important because it had twenty four official lawgivers, twice the usual number. When Danish independence ended the town became the administration centre of Granta-bricshire, and a fortified burh in Edgar's reign (959-75). It was important as a hundred court, having also a market and a mint.

One chronicler says the ditch was made by King John in 1215, and developed in 1267 by Henry III, who intended to build a wall in addition, but this project was not carried out. Fuller says, "Only the south and east of the town lay open, which the King intended to fortify. In order where-unto he built two gates, Trumpington Gate by St Peter's Church; Barnwell Gate by St Andrew's Church. And because gates without walls are but compliments in matter of strength, he intended to wall the town about, if time permitted him. Meantime he drew a deep ditch (called King's Ditch at this day), round about the south and east parts of Cambridge. Presently news is brought to him, that Gilbert, earl of Clare, had seized on the chief city of the realm. No policy for the King to keep Cambridge and lose London the while. Thither marched he in all haste with his army, and may be said to carry the walls of Cambridge away with him, the design thereof sinking at his departure. The town then being unguarded, the insurgents from the Isle of Ely came in number and burnt the King's gates down."

The King's Ditch ran from the Mill Pool in the west, up Mill Lane to Trumpington Street, where it was crossed by a bridge with a gate on it called Trumpington Gate. The ditch continued down Pembroke Street, then taking a diagonal direction down Tibb's Row to St Andrew's Street and Hobson Street. A second bridge crossed the ditch here and had on top a gate called Barnwell Gate. The ditch continued down Jesus Lane, and along Park Street to rejoin the river.

The Ditch, surveyed in 1629, showed a depth variation of from 20 to 180 feet. Of little defensive use, the ditch became instead a nuisance to the town

Near here, east of Magdalen Bridge, the northern end of the King's Ditch would have rejoined the River Cam.

because of the rubbish thrown into it. When Dr Perne, Master of Peterhouse, wrote to the Chancellor of the University in 1574, about the plague, he blamed in part, the King's Ditch. "The other cause, as I conjecture, is the corruption of the King's dycth." So water was diverted to run through the ditch in 1610 and one wonders why thirty years passed and if too many of the workmen died of plague to do the necessary work? When it was cleaned it was not done properly, because the "bed of the ditch was so irregular and the depth varied so much that the water did not flow quickly." The diagram which accompanied the survey is fairly incomprehensible, therefore I have prepared my own simplified version.

The colleges of Cambridge, so well known the world over, grew up on the edges of the medieval town, much of which was destroyed to make way for them. The city has also suffered destruction from modern development and much of history and pre-history still lies beneath the soil and beneath buildings both ancient and modern.

Cambridge seems in so many ways to be an enigma: lived in a million years ago, and continuously occupied for well over two thousand years. Yet much of its mystery remains unsolved, perhaps for all time. If it was habitable a million years ago, why then was it a mere staging post in Roman times? Was it *only* because Cambridge missed Roman "glory" by the mere eight miles by which it stood separated from Ermine Street to the west, which grandly swept its way north and south?

Its origin as a medieval town and its growth as such was largely due to its siting in a fertile region with natural resources. Its river was navigable and its water supply from wells was good, and the part of the town which grew up within the loop of the river was easy to defend with ditches. It had access to the sea via the river, and the mainland route from East Anglia to the Midlands. The advantages would not have been any less in Roman times than in medieval times, yet it was not a great Roman town. Probably the distance from Colchester (Camulodunum), to Cambridge was too small to warrant another principal Roman town being either needed or built.

On the Cam, east of Magdalen Bridge, one can still guess at where the King's Ditch joined the river in the north, if one follows a map, although there are no signs to mark the spot. One will not find the Barnwell Gate or Trumpington Gate, but it is not difficult to find out where they formerly stood. At the bottom of Mill Lane is the pool where the Ditch joined the Cam at its southernmost point. Despite modern development Cambridge is still delightful and many a pleasant hour may be passed in the city, tracing ancient defence lines.

*   *   *   *   *

Godmanchester

Godmanchester stands directly on Ermine Street which originally led from the Thames Bridge in London, through a gate at Bishopsgate to Braughing, Royston, Godmanchester, past Alconbury Hill, Stamford, Ancaster, Lincoln and finally to York. The old North Road is marked by the roadside — no misnomer here. At Claxton the sign changes to Ermine Way. Great gnarled half dead oaks line the way, speaking of antiquity. Ermine Way gives place to Ermine Street.

Ermine Street which once swept through Godmanchester with nothing to deter it except the South Gate, now meets the blankness of a block of flats named Roman Gate, an historic reminder in name only as I consider them drab, dull-bricked and uninteresting. The earlier Roman Gate must have been more beautiful, elegant or at least more interesting than today's replacement. London Street travels to the left, Ermine Street to the right.

Following the direction of the former Roman town wall from south to north one comes to the Causeway, the Ouse and the town beside which stands a white wooden Chinese bridge. Snails, *Arianta arnustorum* and *Cepoea nemoralis*, along with tree roots discovered during exacavation in the Causeway area, prove it to have been a damp, wooded place stretching to the river's edge.

Staggered trenches dug in 1957 at the rear boundaries of buildings on the eastern side of the Causeway, at right angles to the supposed defence line, showed what appeared to be the line of the Roman town wall in the west. The Causeway was a garbage dump in Roman times, because of the many finds — a burnt coin of Aurelian days, a buckle, an enamelled object, a broken opaque ring and pits with skeletons of new-born babies, have all been unearthed.

19

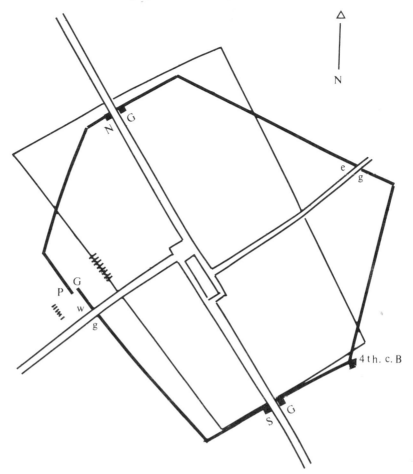

Plan of Roman Godmanchester defences based on the work H.J.M. Green. Thin rectangular lines show second century Roman dyke while the hexagon of thicker lines represents fourth century wall outline; the main compass point gates (NG-North Gate, SG-South Gate, eg-East Gate, wg-West Gate) are shown and in the west a postern gate (PG); ditches and fourth century bastion (4th cB). Road between North and South Gates is Ermine Street.

Known as Duraliponte in Richard of Cirencester's Itinerary III, and in the 9th Antonine Itinerary as Duropipontem,* Durosiponte signifies a bridge over the Ouse. Wherever there was a river and a settlement of people, for one reason or another they would want to cross, so bridges were built. One wonders what kind of bridge the Romans erected and whether it stood at the same place as the bridge today. Coins of Augustus, Tiberius, Claudius, Nero, Vespasian, Trajan and Hadrian, along with such finds as pottery, fragments of

*Chapter Two of 1821 *History of Godmanchester* by R. Fox is headed "Godmanchester — the Durolipons of the Romans". Sir R. Cotton in an article in J. Speed's *Theatre of the Empire of Great Britain* of 1611 said "for certain it was that Roman station Durosipont of the Bridges". Camden Britannia (1586) said "It was the Duroliponte of Richard of Circencester". In a later, the third, Itinerary Richard of Cirencester calls it Duraliponte. The ninth Antonine Itinerary named it Durolipontem.

In spite of the present or past names of the River at Cambridge it is and was part of the Ouse so both Cambridge and Godmanchester would have had bridges over the Ouse.

Roman glass jars, bronze pins and keys tell us Godmanchester was well known to the Romans, and they too must have needed to cross the river. It would appear that the name might have come from a bridge already in existence when the Romans arrived.

Beside the Chinese Bridge, the one time Town Hall records on a black board mounted on its wall, the following legend:

County Record Office

Pepys' House, Brampton 1 mile.

Chartered by King John 1211.

Became Borough in 1604.

Medieval Church.

Queen Elizabeth Grammar School c. 1560.

Chinese Bridge and Waterways of the Old Corn Mill.

17th c. domestic architecture.

Stone Bridge built 1332.

When Caesar visited our shores the Iceni occupied much of Cambridgeshire, Huntingdonshire, Norfolk and Suffolk. The Cambrian Register says the word is derived from Cyn, meaning first, ahead, foremost. So the people were called Cyni, Cyniad, Cynion, with y prefixed, Y-ceni, the foremost tribe. Historians suggest that the Iceni, a powerful Celtic tribe, probably had a settlement at Godmanchester. No doubt the Iceni would have made their settlements near trackways, so they were able to communicate easily with other tribes and make use of the opportunity for barter. Not only that, the area had abundant pasturage, woodlands and water, all necessities of life even in those ancient days. If the Iceni did have a settlement there, then Boadicea no doubt knew the town. Diocletian speaks of her thus: "Bodicca is represented as a tall woman, of remarkable beauty, and the most dignified deportment, with a commanding severity in her countenance, a loud shrill voice, and a great quantity of yellow hair that flowed down to her loins. She wore a massy golden chain about her neck, a flowing robe of various colours, over which was thrown a mantle of coarser stuff. She held a spear in her hand, and from a throne of turf harangued her army, recapitulating the wrongs they had suffered from the Romans."

Known to historians and archaeologists as a Romano-British settlement Godmanchester was always thought to be unwalled. Excavations have however proved beyond all doubt that it was a walled enclosure of some 20 acres, in an irregular hexagonal shape. The wall was backed by a clay rampart with a drainage ditch at the town edge of the rampart. This was of masonry with Barnack ragstone. A concrete mass found by excavation at the west end of east street may have been part of a north-west bastion. When an inn (*mansio*) was built, circa A.D.120, part of the west side of the town was cleared, then a V-shaped ditch was dug round the town for security. The wattle revetment of

Earning Street facing east in the direction of the former fourth century bastion at Godmanchester.

the ditch sides were found later during excavations. The ditch in the north had the remains of wood piles probably indicating a former bridge crossing Ermine Street. Part of the wall at least was accompanied by three steep-sided ditches.

Sewer trenches were dug in 1956 around the town. At that time "footings of a town wall with the ditches in front and a large masonry structure of uncertain character behind,"* were discovered. But certainly today no vallum or fosse can be seen. Because of these findings more excavations were carried out in 1959 by C. Green for the Ministry of Works. This was done at sites adjoining Earning Street and Piper's Lane. The Roman wall which was discovered in 1957 was a mass of Roman-type concrete ten feet wide by one foot thick and four feet below the surface. The section of wall found in 1959 was Barnack limestone rubble, silso sandstone, with large flints and tiles set in cream-coloured mortar. Probably the wall was reveted at the back with earth. Carbon testing of fragments by Davis Vaughan of the Royal Institute dates the wall as between A.D. 230 and 320, most probably A.D. 275 being the date of the building of the defences. The south gate was excavated in 1959-61, the part of the north gate in 1972-3. The gates probably had central carriageways with footways at the outside edges. Originally the gateway "gap" was twice the final width, this gap being partly closed when the later gate towers were added. There would most likely have been a guard house built on the first

*H. J. M. Green — Roman Godmanchester in Proceedings of the Cambridge Antiquarian Society Volume 54, 1961.

floor. No signs of either east or west gates have been found to date. Carbon dating, and a coin dated A.D.270-3 of Tetricus, suggests the date for the building of Godmanchester walls. Excavational evidence of 1973 showed a fan-shaped bastion was built during the late fourth century on to the existing wall in the south east corner. Bastions such as this one were added at a time when they were required to provide a mounting for ballistae.

On the hills to the south of the Roman town of Godmanchester there was a watch-tower or beacon. A close nearby was for centuries called the Beaconfield in the Court Rolls of the Borough. From the watch tower a view of the country could be commanded giving sufficient time to call up troops to any point in danger of attack. The town was near an angle of the river, giving natural fortifications and also at the junction of these three principal roads.

Small Roman towns like Godmanchester were defended with walls at the will of the Imperial Government, for the local Romans did not decide on the defence of their towns. The defences were only built if there was a threat from the enemies of Rome, and these defences would certainly not have been provided if they were likely to have been used against the Roman masters. At one time there was a military fort in the centre of what later became a small Roman walled town. The fort had twin ditches with a rampart and there was also a ravelin. When the rampart was excavated it was proved that there had been post hole settings for a timber revetment. To the east of the site the discovery of four post holes indicated that the bank and ditches were further defended by a timber fort. This early fort was built before Ermine Street was laid.

When Edward the Elder succeeded on the death of King Alfred (899), the title was disputed by Ethelwald, the son of Alfred's eldest brother. Ethelwald joined forces with the Northumbrian Danes and, joined with the East Anglian and Mercian Danes, was proclaimed king. Edward took an expedition to East Anglia and Mercia where Ethelwald was killed and the Danes subjected to the rightful king. The Danes however made piratical skirmishes and encounters with the Saxons so that eventually Edward occupied East Anglia, Northumbria and Mercia, building nine castles, which he garrisoned for defence. Huntingdon already having a castle took over dominance from Godmanchester which was without one.

Godmanchester became a Danish station of defence under Guthrum the Danish leader who established a camp at Cambridge, fighting against King Alfred c. A.D. 875. With the continual arrival of formidable Danes, the Saxons became disheartened and either retired into Wales or submitted to the Danish conquerors. King Alfred, after defeat in January 878, sought refuge in the marshes of the River Parratt, near Bridgewater. He secretly collected many of his supporters and eventually overthrew Guthrum and the other conquering Danes. Guthrum converted to Christianity and entered into a treaty of alliance

The site of North Gate, Godmanchester

with Alfred and was granted vice-royalty over East Anglia and large territories in the north.

Guthrum took possession of the East Angles in 880 (*Anglo-Saxon Chronicle 879*), and at this time a Danish settlement was made at Godmanchester. Camden said "the town from Gorman's camp first took its name". So Roman Durolipons became Gorman-castria and, being suitable, became an important encampment, protected on south and south east by high hills, and on west, north and north west by the Ouse, which separated it from the kingdom of Mercia. After twelve years reign Guthrum died and Godmanchester became a frontier town continually harrassed by the Danes, but after the building of Edward's castle in 917 at Huntingdon, there is no record of local incidents. This castle stood back from Ermine Street, allowing for a barbican or outwork for defence of its principal entrance. In the eleventh century called Godmundcestre, in the twelfth century Gudmencestre, Gumencestre, Guncestre, Gumecestre; in the thirteenth century Gurmudcestre and, since the fourteenth century, named as we know it today.

Godmanchester long ago boasted that it had formerly received kings on their progress with a pageant of nine score ploughs. During the mid-fourteenth century a town ditch, 35 feet wide, was dug, destroying most of the Roman ditch. Godmanchester was thought to be a market town though there is little evidence of an early market. Modern street maps preserve the early hexagonal plan. Today the small town is delightful with an air of calm and peace now that the Huntingdon bypass has diverted much of the traffic from its streets.

*   *   *   *   *

Great Chesterford

Continuing the spiral direction of the web from Cambridge and leaving Godmanchester, Great Chesterford is about 7 miles south east of the web centre. Great Chesterford in Essex is the only town in the county apart from Colchester definitely known to be walled, but its ancient name is unknown.

Belgic Iron Age dyke defences found at this small town point to its antiquity and class it in the category of Oppida. Oppidum meant quite literally a town, although Roman historians were not always accurate in the use of the word, often using it for a very minor settlement; for a series of dykes surrounding an enclosed area; or for hill forts, but in this case it meant a town.

During the early eighteenth century the town wall could still be seen, but after that the wall was continually robbed for road-mending purposes. Stukely visited Great Chesterford in July 1719, and mentioned walking on the Roman walls still visible above ground. Antiquarian that he was, he was disgusted at the way the people were mending highways with stones from the ancient walls.

Joseph Strutt examined the walls in 1172-3. "I had an opportunity of scrutinising into the...solid foundations, composed of rag stones and strong cement; this wall full 3ft. in height...and on this was built the wall, composed of rubble, stone and cement, together with layers of bricks." The walls were 12 feet thick and upwards of 1000 feet in length so that Great Chesterford could not have been a small station.

R. C. Neville, later Lord Braybrooke, excavated Great Chesterford from 1845 to about 1860, but some of his findings are vague and inaccurate. Excavations by the Ministry of Works in 1948-9 identified the wall, but show Neville's map to be incorrect as far as direction is concerned. The long axis of the wall runs north-west to south-east but Neville put it as north to south. The excavations indicated that the walls were erected some time during the fourth century. The area enclosed by walls was about 36 acres, divided into northern and southern regions by a tributary of the Cam. No towers or bastions are known to have existed but there was a ditch outside the walls. During the excavation the site of the North Gate was found. There were apparently three phases in building or re-building the North Gate, but insufficient evidence by excavation exists to say what these three stages mean. However, Great Chesterford is very important to archaeologists.

The true dimensions of the town wall are not known, although the dig of 1948 revealed that the foundation trench would have carried a 12 foot masonry wall. Pottery buried beneath the trench was known to be dated at the end of the second century. Third and fourth century finds show the town wall not to have been built before 300 A.D. Coins of the period of Constantine (306-27) were also unearthed.

Great Chesterford was important as a Roman military station because it was placed at a point in the north which controlled the Stort-Essex-Cam Valley, and more importantly, the Icknield Way. An early Roman fort was built here, the southern military ditch being discovered in 1948-9 some yards north of the North Gate of the later Roman walled town. The fort stood on

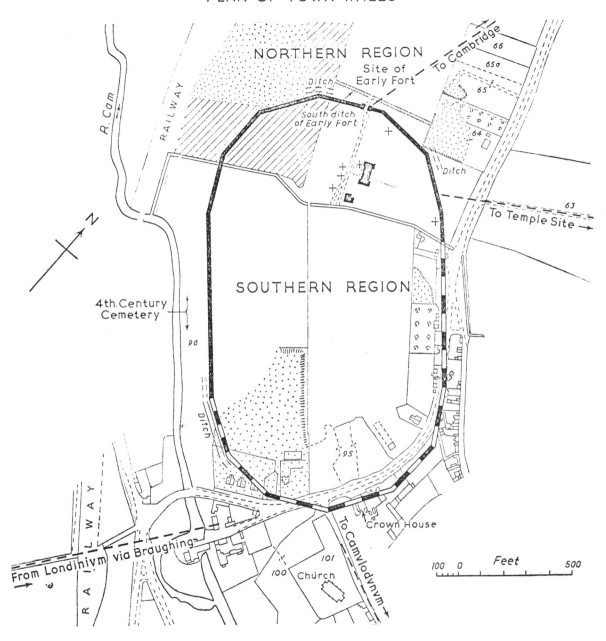

GREAT CHESTERFORD
PLAN OF TOWN WALLS

NORTHERN REGION

Site of
Early Fort

To Cambridge

66

65a

65

Ditch

South ditch
of Early Fort

64

Ditch

To Temple Site →

63

R. Cam

RAILWAY

N

SOUTHERN REGION

4th. Century
Cemetery

90

Ditch

95

From Londinivm via Braughing

RAILWAY

To Camvlodvnvm →

Crown House

101

100

Church

100   0   Feet   500

Excavations of 1948-9 identified the Great Chesterford Town Wall shown in solid black, which
was erected some time during the fourth century.

Great Chesterford streets today are lined with charming elegant houses, half-timbered and decorated with hanging baskets.

high ground above the river, where the main road now lies. The ditch itself, six feet deep and thirteen feet wide, was of the size associated with permanent defences. According to pottery finds at the excavation, the ditch was an early one. A Roman road led north from London via Braughing to Great Chesterford, going right through the centre of the Roman town, entering via the South Gate and leaving by the North Gate in a north-easterly direction.

Beyond the railway station, well outside the present town, crossed by a mere trickle from the Cam, hidden under grass, buried under farm fields, lie the remains of the one-time Roman town. No part of its hidden life or walls remains in view to remind one of the town's old sorrows or glories.

*   *   *   *   *

Bedford

Some 30 miles west of Great Chesterford is the town of Bedford, the next strand in the web. Early Bedford was possibly settled by the course of the river Ouse which made a wide sweep south forming an important defensive boundary at a time when much of this district was low-lying swamp and forest. This early settlement was at a place near the river where it was easy to cross, and where it was possible to provide some kind of early defensive system.

The town appears to have been inhabited in Romano-British times probably as an unenclosed settlement. Its name then is not known and there is no proof that there was ever a permanent Roman settlement.

Like other ancient places Bedford's name was spelt in numerous ways, Bedcanfords, Bedanforda, Bedeforda, Biedcanforda, Beidforda, Bedeforda and so on. The town was first mentioned in 571 when Cuthwulf defeated the Britons there. Subsequently it became a Danish borough which was captured in 914 by Edward the Elder.

Bedicanford is made up of three Celtic words - Bad (a boat), Can (with or by), and Ford (a passage by water). This certainly is confirmed by its position. In fact the *Anglo-Saxon Chronicle* specifically states that the Saxons "took Bedicanford," the inference being that they found it already called by that name. Later the name changed to Beda (Bada-war) and ford (passage through a stream), so as the place was fortified on the north bank, the name meant the fortress on the ferry.

Very little seems to be known about Bedford defences and certainly nothing of them remains today. But one chronicler of history tells us that King Edward "went with the army to Bedanfords and gained the burgh, and he remained there 4 weeks and commanded the burg on the south of the river to be built (atimbran) before he went thence," in 915. He also ordered a new town to be built on the south side of the river. It was enclosed by a ditch. Previous to that date the town, with whatever fortifications commanded the ford, was on the north side. An ancient cutting once described a circuit from a point on the river to the west of the town, to a point on the east and would no doubt be Edward's project. Some traces of an interior rampart are still visible beside part of the ditch although much of the ditch itself has completely vanished. The cutting is called the King's Ditch and when stockaded would form an effective defence for Edward's new garrison.

The *Anglo-Saxon Chronicle* says that "in 917 before Easter (13th April) the King came again with his army from Huntingdon and East Anglia. They made a fortress at Tempsford abandoning the one at Huntingdon. They went till they reached Bedford; and the men who were inside went out against them, and fought against them and put them to flight and killed a good part of them." Two years later the Danes again besieged Bedford but "men of Bedford went out and routed them with great slaughter."

Bedford also had a castle, probably erected in the reign of William II (1087-1100), having a round keep of timber stockading surmounted on an earthen mound with a surrounding fosse combined with an outer wooden defence. This was a typical Norman castle. By the reign of Henry I or Stephen the wooden stockades were replaced by stone from the belt of limestone north of Bedfordshire.

The six maps on the left show the growth of one defended area, Bedford, throughout nine hundred years. Map I and II show the Saxon Baeda's ford and the defensive bank, ditch and Mikesgate of 1060; Maps III and IV define the King's Ditck (sic) of the thirteenth century and the same ditch in 1600 with three bridges spanning the stream; V is a map of 1765 marking the ditch with dots only, while VI, of 1807, shows the ditch with roads crossing it at three points.

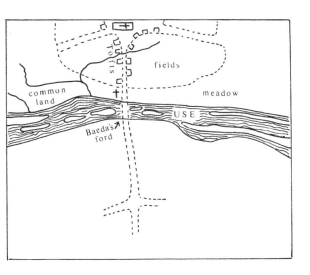

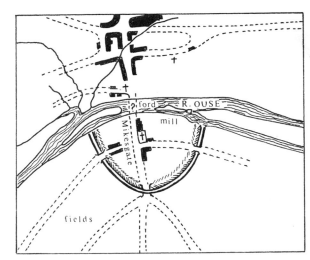

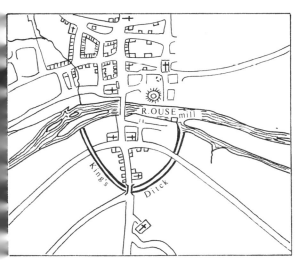

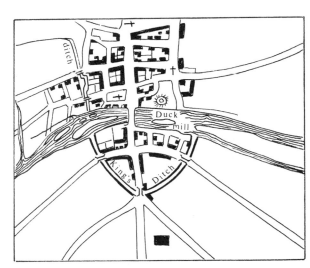

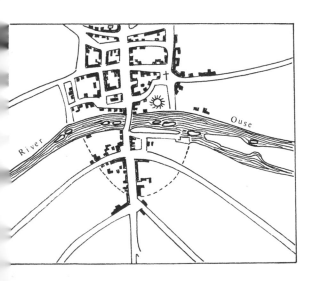

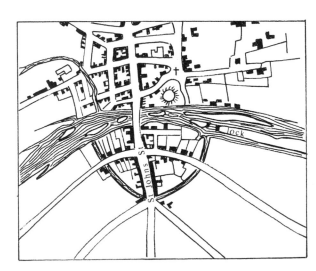

Hugh de Beauchamp was the first occupier of Bedford castle, installed by William II as the Keeper of the Castle. He was succeeded by Simon his son and later by Miles, the nephew of Simon. The latter were probably responsible for the stone defences.

When William de Beauchamp rebelled against King John the castle was given to Falkes de Breaute who strengthened the castle with towers and outer defences and added engines of war, and surrounded the whole with deep moats which were probably dry ones. De Breaute, a Norman mercenary, had risen to power as a local servant during the civil wars at the end of the King's reign and became sheriff of seven counties.

Eventually his ill deeds caught up with him; so many complaints were lodged against his actions that he was called to come before three justices to answer the charges. He retaliated by ordering the capture of these three men, saying they were to be imprisoned in his castle. Leaving his brother William in comand of Bedford castle, he went post haste to Wales to enlist help. The king ordered William to surrender the castle but received only refusal. The church then excommunicated the de Breautes and all inside the castle, and it is reported that the King "swore a mighty oath by the soul of his father that he would hang all who were taken when the castle fell." In 1224 the king assembled a large force and with siege equipment converged on the castle. Many towns contributed men and equipment to the king and Corfe castle alone sent 25,000 crossbows. The siege began on 20th June and the barbican was taken, the walls breached and the outer bailey fell. While crossbowmen showered arrows on the besieged from a belfrois, miners undermined the walls. On 14th August the keep was fired causing great gaps to appear in it and the castle fell. The King, true to his word, hanged a number of men but three were cut down before they were dead. The castle was razed to the ground. Falkes was discovered near Chester and ordered to attend his castle at Bedford, which he did to find his brother and friends dead. He was given absolution but banished from the realm and two years later is said to have died of poisoned fish in St Ciriac. A descendant of the original de Beauchamp, William almost totally demolished the castle remains after the siege. The outer bailey walls were knocked down and the inner bailey was reduced to half the height.

The King's Ditch may be traced today by anyone willing to spend time walking and searching with a map. A small car park beside the Ouse at Duckmill Lane is situated beside a footbridge leading across the river. From this side, north, one may see the entrance or exit of a small stream. Well hidden behind trees is this narrow strip of water, all that remains of a once much wider defensive ditch. Retracing steps back across the bridge and turning left under a small footbridge called King's Ditch Bridge the stream flows on. Behind the bridge the stream drifts partly through and partly under the buildings of the Dame Alice Harpur School.

A narrow strip of rough woodland shades and hides the trickle of water beside part of the defensive bank in the grounds of an old people's housing settlement at Bedford.

The ditch is then piped under Cardington Road. Beyond the footpath the King's Ditch is a brook some 3 feet wide, protected by a brick wall on one side and a bank on the other. The brook may be followed by walking over grass and under trees in the grounds of an old people's housing settlement, this is the same ditch. Further on a narrow strip of rough woodland shades the trickle of water. On the opposite side, gardens back onto the ditch. On the near side, as the ditch curves round in an arc, the height of the bank rises showing that it is indeed a defensive bank.

Finally the ditch disappears from sight, piped underground at the massive roundabout which lies at the bottom of Kingsway. Through pipes it flows to join the River Ouse on the site of County Hall. Hidden, picturesque, behind brambles and bushes, covered with green slime and pond weed; cluttered by fallen trees, old tin baths, bicycle wheels, and general flotsam and jetsam — an ignominious end to the King's Ditch. However the pool is said not to be part of the old ditch, although one would think the water may come from the same source.

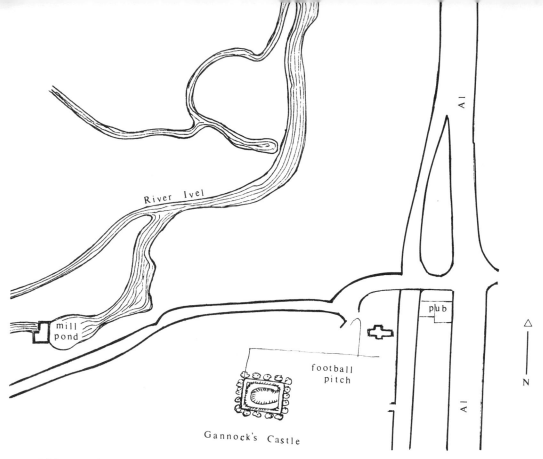

This map shows Gannock's Castle, Tempsford, in relation to the A1 and the River Ivel.

Tempsford

Temps is the Danish Saga name for Thames, indicating that the Ouse on which Tempsford now stands was known as the Thames to the Anglo-Saxons. Temesfords, Tamise-fords in the tenth/eleventh century; Tamisford in the twelfth century; Temysford in the fourteenth century and now Tempsford, retaining its ancient former name.

In 921 the Danes set out up river from Bedford to Tempsford, where they "wrought a work" and settled into their new headquarters, so says an old record. During the war between the Danes and England, circa 917, the Danes invaded Huntingdon and Bedfordshire, then in English hands. The Danes built their new fort at Tempsford in 921 on the River Ivel, a tributary which joins the Ouse at Tempsford which they proposed to use as a base instead of Huntingdon. The occupation of Tempsford was a military success gained by an effort in which as least five of their armies took part. That same summer King Edward's army marched to Tempsford and took the fortress by storm.

In 878 King Alfred defeated the attacking Danes under their leader Guthrum. This led to peace when he offered to cede to the Danes, at the Treaty of Wedmore in the same year, the northern part of his country provided they became Christian. They accepted and settled in their own kingdom called the Danelaw. Alfred trained armies to protect his kingdom; had ships built to fight the Danes on the sea and had many monasteries and churches restored before he died in 901.

By 978 a further flood of Danes invaded the land. Then King Ethelred, the Redeless or ill-advised, tried to buy peace with the Danes. Dane-geld or Dane-gold was paid to the invaders but always the Danes returned to attack. Foolishly Ethelred had the peaceful Danes who lived all those years in the Danelaw attacked and hundreds of men, women and children were slain. Among the dead was Gunhilda, King Sweyn of Denmark's sister. This happened on St Brice's Day 1002. Sweyn invaded Britain with a large army to avenge the Massacre of St Brice's Day and Ethelred's wife fled to Normandy, her former home, with their son Edward. Soon afterwards Ethelred died. For many years the Danes overran the whole of East Anglia and in 1010 they burnt Tempsford.

On the death of Sweyn his son Canute became the Danish leader, and finally King of England in 1016. It was under Canute, a Christian, strong and just man, that England was divided into four great districts or earldoms — Northumbria, Mercia, East Anglia and Wessex. During this time Tempsford's defences were at the height of their power. Canute's greatest gift to the people of England was peace. With his reign began a peace virtually unbroken for nearly two hundred years.

Though the burh at Tempsford was occupied by the Danes, the earthwork may be of earlier date because Danish earthworks were never rectangular. The fort is usually said to be Gannock's Castle, having an oblong central platform 120 feet by 80 feet. This was surrounded by a strong inner rampart and a moat 20 feet wide in places, lying south west of the village, some 200 yards from a former artificial loop of the main stream once used as a mill leat, near one of the ancient tracks or roadways, it possessed a circular mound inside the rectangular earthwork. Tempsford today is situated upon the right bank of the Ivel. Within the north east angle of Tempsford encampment Gannock Castle stands. There are no signs of masonry, but the word "castle" was commonly applied to places where no stone buildings were ever built.

The entrance to the early defence was from the north east angle by the small circular mound on the rampart. This rampart was surrounded by a small bank which "may have been the base of a stockaded tower." Formerly the surrounding fields were said to be scored with traces of lines outside the encampment. If they existed, they are obliterated now. The Great North

Road once ran straight through the village, but a by-pass has left it in peace.

Researching mounds and fortifications does not necessarily imply that one finds what one is looking for—on the contrary, but sometimes this has its funny side. Journeying to Tempsford I entered the village in search of a mound 80 feet high. The mound was nowhere to be seen. Thinking it might be further out of the village than I had expected—maps and distances can be deceptive—I drove out of the village across the main road, finally asking again at a village post office. No one had heard of Tempsford Mound. This seemed very strange. Enquiring at an estate office I was directed to an old army camp where the estate manager assured me there was an old moat inside the grounds of the camp. I never found it. Taking refuge and coffee back in a Tempsford pub I asked the landlord, who although resident there only a few months, knew the facts. The defence was on the other side of the village street, at the edge of a field and the figure 80 feet was one of width, not height.

Anyone visiting Gannock's (or Cannock's) Castle today will have to walk to the far end of Tempsford football pitch. There in among a clump of trees, behind the far goal post, lies history. History difficult to find hidden behind nettles, brambles and bushes. Here surrounded by a damp moat(there is hardly enough water to call it wet), are the remains of the Tempsford defences. It is possible to cross to the mound by walking across fallen trees, but this is only to be advised for devotees of archaeology or adventurous children. Somewhere nearby, outside the village near Goldington, a bridge was the traditional site of the battle, known as "Bloody Battle" bridge. Now Tempsford is almost by-passed by life as well as the main road except, that is, for its shining white houses, its few villagers, the sound of a football in the field beside Gannock's Castle, the quiet moat which has been there a thousand years, and cabbage white butterflies in the far field.

A damp moat, the remains of Tempsford defences.

3. Land of The Iceni

KING'S LYNN — CASTLE ACRE — NORWICH — CAISTOR ST EDMUNDS — NEW BUCKENHAM

King's Lynn

IN THE days of the earliest settlers of King's Lynn, rude wattle huts were built on almost inaccessible islets in the treacherous Linn swamps. They needed no forts because no one could reach them. This burh of Linn was a defence in itself having a treacherous seaboard to the north, along with an artificial embankment with its accompanying ditch. Water diverted from the Gaywood river in the south formed a moated protection in the east, while arms of the sea defended the burh to the west.

Among the early settlers were the Iceni who, isolated by the dense forest which covered central East Anglia, used the Icknield Way, the Peddars Way, and the rivers to move about their territory, but movement was not easy. With the coming of the Romans and the building of roads, East Anglia was opened up for the ancient tribes as well as for the Romans. The Romans are thought to have had ferries running across the Wash and are known to have made use of existing resources. It is quite probable that Boadicea used the Lynn/Wash area, before the time of the Romans. She would have passed through Castle Acre and possibly through Norwich on her way across her tribal lands, for this area north of the forest was where her tribe had easiest access.

Under Bishop Turbus, who died in 1174, much land was reclaimed from the sea. It was then that a rude wall of banks and ditches was built in two almost parallel lines, about 300 yards apart. The southern bank ran along the River Mill, while the northern bank followed the left bank of the Purfleet, the name probably meaning principal stream. These two banks ran seaward and were strengthened by tree trunks placed vertically side by side as a stockade. Both rivers have now disappeared but are remembered in name. At that time the town was known as Bishop's Lin. With the east and west banks, the whole enclosed an irregular parallelogram. The name Lin or Lun may be a Celtic word meaning a pond.

The South Gate at King's Lynn from the outside with aslar stone facing; inside the surface is brick.

St Ann's Fort Ruins, King's Lynn, from the land side, inside the Dock yard.

The banks were raised to protect the community from the inroads of the sea. Banks or ramparts, often called walls from the Latin *uall-um,* a rampart, and not to be confused with stone walls. These earthworks were probably made in 1250-1337 when the town was at its peak of trade.

The Briggate, a western parallel with the Gannock, was the byrig or earthwork. Byrig-gate became Brig-gate, which means the road along the rampart or earthwork. It corresponds with our present word High Street, a name intensely suggestive, quite literally meaning high.

The Stonegate was built to protect the town from tidal surges when high banks were thrown up along the Millflett, first called Mill-byrig, then Stone-byrig. These are now replaced by roads named Stonegate Street and Millfleet. Stonegate was the name given by the Danes who later lived here, gate to them meaning road or way.

At the beginning of the thirteenth century the town was defended by four wooden towers or block-houses, the north, south, east and west bretasks. The north bretask of 1270 was styled "Bretask of the Bishop." The west bretask site is not known exactly, but it was near a water-gate, probably near the mouth of the Purfleet. The watch towers are not mentioned after the time of Richard II. Portable wooden towers were also used which could be kept in reserve and erected when needed. In 1298, the tallage, which Benedict de Weasenham ought to have paid to the community, was remitted, in lieu of the rent he sacrificed in storing a timber bretask for eighteen months. The walls of King's Lynn were once defended with nine bastion towers or projecting buttresses; two towers only have their names recorded, the White Tower and the Black Tower.

In the middle of the fourteenth century the ditches were repeatedly scoured or recast, the surrounding walls and earthworks repaired and gates strengthened to assist in repelling an assault, particularly during the wars with France and Scotland.

The Stone Wall at Kettlewell Lane, built between 1300 and 1375, consists of flints, clunch and flat bricks. Ramparts or battlements have gone and only five buttresses remain. Each arch on the inner side was provided with a loophole for the cross bow, and a step on which the soldier might place his knee, when aiming at an approaching foe. In times of great emergency, the gates would be closed and built up with stone and lime; a huge earthwork would be thrown up along the whole line of the fortifications, hiding arches and gateways. On top of the temporary earthwork watch and ward was rigidly kept. Along battlements pieces of artillery were placed, and assaulting parties repulsed and their scaling ladders hauled back into the moat waters. In the time of Henry VIII all the gardens in Lynn were destroyed in order to obtain sufficient earth to revet the walls. The arches are now three to five feet high inside, showing the present road is considerably higher than before. The ground outside the wall is some four to five feet lower than it is inside. Originally these arches would have been nine to ten feet high. This wall was the only stone wall built in King's Lynn, except for an insignificant curtain on both sides of the Gannock Gate. It was often repaired, strengthened and re-cast, but never enlarged in any way. It seems that money ran out when the walls were being built or more of the town would have been enclosed. Poor quality stone supports the theory of lack of money. In spite of this King John, when harassed by the barons, sought refuge in King's Lynn.

Where the East Gate once stood, at the junction of Littleport Street and Kettlewell Lane, the latter continues as Wyatt Street. The side wall of *The-Hob-in-the-Wall* shows many traces of the old town walls among the modern-day brick. There are traces here of three arch tops at ground level, and the wall about ten feet high continues, much repaired along Wyatt Street, and eight bricked-in segmented pointed arches show low down on the wall. Near the bend in this street are still traces of the Gaywood, the waters of which were once part of the protective water-filled ditch which surrounded the town to north, south and west.

In 1520 the King's commissioners received instructions to fortify the town, in order to resist the landing of a hostile force, in case such an event should occur. The new gate defending the road to London, the south entrance to the burh, was completed and provided with a drawbridge and portcullis, but much remained to be done to make the town defensible.

The Cromwellian Major-General Edward Montague, Earl of Manchester, arrived at Lynn in 1642 and demanded that it surrender; this was rejected so on 28th August the town came under siege. By 15th September some of the townsmen came out and began to cut the banks; this flooded all routes in and out of the town. The shrieks and cries of women and children were audible well outside the town. Many had been killed by the attackers' gun fire and now the fresh water supply had been cut off from outside. The townspeople also felled all the trees near the town to remove a covered approach for the Earl's army. Their efforts were to no avail as when another demand to surrender came the next day they surrendered without bloodshed. In 1643 the King entered Lynn by the East Gate and the town declared in his favour.

The present South Gate is of brick, with ashlar stone facing on the outside front face and probably made or refaced in 1520. The walls and turrets were crenellated. In each of the north and south walls there are three merlons, while the side walls to east and west each have much longer merlon finishing in embrasures at the ends. The south face crenellations are of stone, the others of brick and stone copings. A chimney stands on the east parapet and there must have been one in the west, for there is a fireplace in the western wall of a room on the middle floor. The gun-ports, simple circular openings, can be clearly seen.

Archaeologists say there were two other South Gates built previously to this one on or near the same site. The present gate house has stairs in the two half octagonal turrets projecting from the south face. The large gateway passing under the edifice rises the whole height of the first two floors. The observant will notice that this passage-way is slightly off centre, nearer the western side. This asymmetry is so cleverly carried out as to be almost unnoticed, certainly it does not give the gate a lop-sided appearance as one might expect.

The room above the main arch housed the portcullis machinery, while the arch itself still has the grooves for the portcullis. There are also the four

Where the East Gate once stood, at the junction of Littleport Street and Kettlewell Lane.

iron hinge pins for the wooden gates. The lower floor of the gate is cut through with two small pedestrian gates, probably nineteenth century. This cutting through would have happened when traffic increases made it expedient to remember travellers on foot. The "new" South Gate, finished in 1520 and built of Barnack stone, is a handsome specimen of sixteenth century defensive architecture. The side arches are but recent additions. Both the eastern and western buttresses of the south face of the gate contained a privy. These are only small closets and it is not unusual to find a garderobe in a buttress in medieval architecture. One writer suggests that formerly a timber palisade was attached to the South Gate.

The East Gate was the second most important entrance and had an efficient drawbridge and was probably crenellated on all four sides. There were two buttresses with many steps and the main arch was sharp pointed and very narrow. This crenellated gate was probably built in Edward III's time, during the fifty years after 1327. The gate was repaired in 1541 with the arms of Henry VIII placed over the archway to "point" a royal borough. It was known also as St Catherine's Gate, the adjoining wall having a chapel dedicated to St Catherine. East Gate was taken down in 1800 because of traffic inconvenience.

Doucehill or Dowshill Gate was near old Fisher Fleet where five hundred years ago the sea came almost up to the gate.

In the east is the Gannock, the oldest bank, probably raised during the twelfth century, which can be easily observed when proceeding along the Wall past Red Mount. The name further perpetuated by Guanock Terrace and Guanock Gate still exists just beyond the Red Mount. There has always been controversy over the meaning of the word. "Gannock was the King's standard and stood at a high point" says one historian. Another puts Gua as being of the same origin as war, and knock as the British for hill. Yet a third, cnoc-knoll and gan-an to go, means Pilgrimage Hill or Perambulation Mound. The latter seems more likely because when the bounds were annually walked on Ascension Day, the people were imitating an ancient feast called Terminalia, which the Romans dedicated to the god Terminus.

The arch on the walls was a postern and being sited on the Gannock was known as Gannock Gate. It was also called the North Gannock Gate, and was built of brick, carstone and limestone. The three main arches are pointed while recess arch heads are segmented which shows they are of later date. Therefore the curtain walls are of later date than the central arches. There was a water-filled ditch behind, and water still flows there freely today.

Old Gannock Gate or South Gannock Gate was also a postern on the Gallows Bank, midway between the Millfleet and South Gate. There was a curtain of stone and brickwork. It had a small squarish gatehouse, with an upper floor while the lower floor had a passage through it. There was also a

This gateway was a postern and, being sited on the Gannock, at King's Lynn, was known as Gannock Gate.

smaller arch either side for pedestrians and an entrance to steps to the first floor. No reference was made to it after the time of Edward III, but the ruins are distinctly shown in Buck's Prospect of 1741. No trace of this gate and curtain wall is in existence now.

St Anne's Fort or St Agnes' Gate was named after a conventual chapel near the mouth of the Purfleet. It was also called the Royal Fortress, and was erected at the time of the Spanish invasion threat of 1588. It was built on the site of a former hermit's cave. The fort had no parapet, it being considered defence enough to use sandbags in time of trouble. It was well positioned because no ship could enter the town except by passing the fort first.

When the French threatened to invade England, ten guns were landed at St Anne's Fort from the Tower of London (1770). The guns were given various names, including St Ann, Queen Boadicea and the Lynn Independent, after a voluntary artillery detachment.

The Red Mount, an octagonal chapel with three storeys, was completed in 1485. The upper is cruciform shaped, of stone with brick at the top, possibly the smallest chapel in England. It once had a flight of stone stairs running towards the internal circumference of the octagonal part. This room was used by the officiating priest. The lower floor, probably the original chapel, shows evidence that it once housed a tomb. The walls on this floor are arched as is the second one, and had a cistern (seemingly added to the building later), probably used for water storage during the Civil War. The chapel had lovely tracery said to be comparable with King's College Chapel, Cambridge.

Red is known to be a corruption of road — perhaps from some ancient road which once crossed the site. At one time it was called Mount Fort because during Charles I's time it was used to store gunpowder. It was also known as Our Lady's Mount.

*　　*　　*　　*　　*

Castle Acre

At Castle Acre the Peddars Way, the once great Roman Road, is crossed by another Roman road beginning at Water Newton (Durobrivae), west of Peterborough, crossing north Norfolk in a large sweeping arc to Smallburgh, and possibly ending at Caister-by-Yarmouth, on the coast two miles from Great Yarmouth. Water Newton was a fortified Roman site with an enclosed area of some 44 acres, with a still visible earth bank which was part of Durobrivae town wall. A Roman milestone found at Water Newton suggests that it might have once been a civitas capital.

Civitas capitae were sometimes established as local government administration centres, often formed from Iron Age tribal groups, using either a village outside a fort or native centre already in use. Quiet Castle Acre village standing at this one-time great crossroads still shows its ancient glory and former importance. Now it is peaceful and quiet with a delightful priory which, to me, compares more than favourably with Fountains Abbey. At the other end of the village, well hidden from the casual eye, the remains of the castle stand sentinel over the Nar valley. In between priory and castle is a one-time Roman encampment. Iron Age finds have been excavated and a Saxon cemetery where there were one hundred burial urns has been discovered. A few miles from Swaffham, north of the River Nar, the village has enormous earthworks which support and surround the castle. These ancient mounds, banks and ditches are said to be part of a great line of inland communications, possibly connected with Boadicea. The site was well chosen with the Nar running from east to west, on its way to the Wash. This east-west inland communication protected by Bichamditch cut across the Roman road, just west of the Icknield Way. Another protection, the Launditch, lay halfway between Castle Acre and Elmham. Here was Iceni territory. The old Castle Acre would have seen a good deal of the traffic of north Norfolk. The village stands at the crossroads leading to the Wash, the north, to Scandinavia, south towards London, east to the coast and the continent of Europe beyond, and west to the centre of Britain.

An archaeologist, Mr Kerrich, whose notebooks are in the British Museum, visited Castle Acre in 1787 and concluded the earthworks were not made by the Normans. Differences in levels of the circular works; the irregularity of the horse shoe work; the walls being built across ditches; all point to the fact that the earthworks were not thrown up for the purpose of building the castle. The largest enclosure, some ten acres, never had a wall and was not included in the Norman castle. The enclosure was once called the barbican, a word generally used for an outwork or covering fortification for a gate. The shape of the wall and bank is Roman and excavations at the time produced Roman urns. Francis Blomefield mentions coins of Vespasian and Constantine as having been found there. The north and south banks incline inwards to join the circular works. He concludes that the circular and horseshoe works are of still earlier construction.

The Roman part of Castle Acre village is curious in shape. The west bank of the large enclosure is quite straight but because of the incline of the south and north banks it is assumed that the Romans chose to include them inside their camp. The north-east enclosure too is probably Roman.

This site, Castle Acre, was granted to William de Warenne, who came over with William the Conqueror. De Warenne married Gundreda, the Conqueror's daughter, and it was de Warenne or his son who built the castle which remained in the family until the fifteenth century when it became derelict. No real date of building has been established, but Gundreda is said to have died at the castle in 1085, though this too is uncertain. This does however give a space of nineteen years during which time the castle would have been erected. A charter of 1135 confirms that the castle was standing when the second Earl of Arundel died there that year. Edward I visited Castle Acre several times during his reign, the last time being in 1297. Fifty years later the castle lay in ruins. Half a century later still the castle ditches were made feeding grounds for cattle at a fee of five shillings per annum!

Coming up into Castle Acre from the Swaffham direction one can easily see where the lower South Gate stood. A high grassy bank to the left is part of a former bank and ditch or walling defence. To the right a flint retaining wall guards a garden where part of the South Gate with its two towers once stood.

Most of the houses on Bailey Street have old stones and flints from the ancient castle wall built into them. The two side streets, both D-shaped, are unchanged from the medieval plan. Backing onto the main street, they have similar cottages and houses, some with garden walls encrusted with Roman bricks, set among flint and modern brick.

Bailey Street runs through the centre of what was once the complete enclosure of the castle and village defended by banks and ditches. In this street lived armourers, labourers, castle dependants and traders.

Bailey Gate, at the north end of the village, is built of rubble, with Barnack stone quoining. The portcullis groove still remains and there was once a room above which held the portcullis machinery and ammunition. Two iron hinge pins which held the gates still jut out some 12 feet up the tower

Modern Castle Acre village and surrounding fields, with castle, earthworks and flat Roman fields, Bailey Street can be seen centre and Bailey Gate centre right.

The Norfolk Archaeological Unit

43

walls. Some nine hundred years after the original castle workers came to live inside the village walls, some villagers are still in the service of the castle, repairing and maintaining the walls.

*　　*　　*　　*　　*

Norwich

The *Monasticon** states that until 1253 Norwich was apparently an open town clustered round a great fortress. Norwich was then surrounded for the first time by a fossa which was the single word for ditch and palisade. A licence was granted by King Henry III to enclose the city with a bank and ditch. The walling of the city was to defend it against the king's enemies and prevent traders entering the city without paying tolls.

Francis Blomefield says the walls were commenced in 1294 and finished in 1319-20. In 1342 the gates and towers were fortified and made fit to dwell in. The circuit of defences took the form of two arcs of walling and two stretches of river enclosing the city. To the north the wall extended from St Martin's at Oak Gate to the river bank on the south side of Pockthorpe Gate. The southern arc ran from the river bank at Carrow to that at New Mills by Heigham Gate. The north-west and the east of Norwich was protected by the River Wensum which was considered defence enough.

The walls were built of flint, stone and rubble, something like 37,000 tons of masonry being used in the building. Beside each gate there were recessed arches with loopholes and above the arcading was a path or wall-walk a yard wide. The walls stood some 18 feet high by 1 yard thick. Where the recesses were made the pillars beside the walls were of greater thickness to provide room for the soldiers in the arches, and add strength to the walls. These great walls included 39 round towers and one polygonal tower. There were 12 gates in all, some flanked with round towers for added defence, while outside the walls a ditch . . . 8 feet deep by 50 to 60 feet wide gave further protection. This defence was considered large in its day, enclosing an area greater than the city of London. The peculiar course of Norwich walls, on both sides of the river, has no parallel in the British Isles.

In the year 1337, a further grant of murage was obtained by the city. The city authorities, in the custom of the day, farmed out the work to Richard Spynk, who could, in exchange, collect the murage tax and keep any profit for himself. Spynk was a benefactor to the city since he made up the deficiency between the actual cost of the walls and the far lower sum which could be collected in murage. For five years he was responsible for the work on the walls and gates, furnishing the latter with the very necessary munitions and machinery of war including 30 espringals each with 100 gorgions and other necessary equipment.

**Monasticon Anglicanum*, by William Dugdale and Roger Dodsworth published in 3 volumes, 1655, 1661 and 1673.

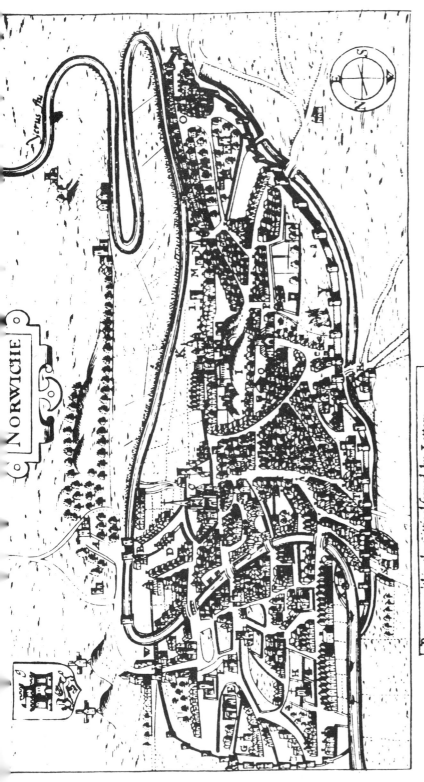

NORWICHE

Places within the Cittie observed by Letters.

A. S. Leonards
B. Bishopps gate
C. The Cathedrall Church
D. S. Martins at ý Pallis gate
E. S. Botholds
F. S. Clements
G. S. Augustins
H. S. Martins at the Oke
I. The Castle
K. S. Peters Permountergate
L. S. Martins on the hill
M. S. Iohns on the hill

N. S. Michaels
O. S. Iohns at the gate
P. S. Stephens
Q. The Market place
R. S. Gyles gate
S. Hell gate.
T. S. Benets gates.
V. S. Stephens gates.
W. Pockthorpe gate.
X. The New Mills.
Y. Chapell in the fieilde.
Z. S. Martins gate.

John Speed's map of Norwich showing the course of the river, how it protected the city in two parts, and the walls and gate and bastion towers, also a two-part defence.

45

The Danes gave the name Cungesford to the part of the city which is today King Street. Here the water defence, at the foot of Carrow Hill, joined the walled defence and gate in the south of the city. Today there is little sign of the former gate but on either side of King Street, the course of the wall lies down one side to the river at Carrow Swing Bridge and, on the other, climbs uphill to Butler's Tower and the Black Tower.

Beside the swing bridge, outside the city limits, two ruined old Boom Towers remain, the former defences of the River Wensum. When necessary the river was closed to traffic by the lowering of a boom or chain stretched over the water from one tower to the other, and the toll collected by the man who lived in the near tower. Dungeons for criminals were built inside the Boom Tower on the far side of the river. Heavily fortified it held a naturally strong position standing alone as it did, with excellent all round visibility. These Boom Towers are unique in Britain, Norwich being the only city which prohibited access to the city by water.

On the hillside by Carrow Bridge, Butler's or Botelier's Tower stands part way up the slope. Inside the wall here a path of steps leads up beside the wall. Outside the wall is another steep slope with some steps which leads to Black Tower at the top of the hill. Black Tower was also known as Governor's Tower as it was a military residence at one period. In 1625 the tower was used for poor plague victims and five years later six houses were built on top of the hill as pest houses. The name Snuff Tower was given when the tower was used as a snuff mill in 1783. Adjoining Black Tower on top of the hill a large section of city wall stands complete with wall walk and recessed loophole arches.

Beyond Black Tower another section of wall stands inside the grounds of a semi-derelict house. The wall may be traced inside some of the houses on Ber Street, the road which joins Carrow Hill.

Ber Street is a wide highway leading nowhere. Proof that this was a Roman road exists, for in 1784 when men were sinking a well in the basement of the Castle, they found a regular beaten Roman footpath used before the hill was thrown up. So in Roman times Ber Street obviously led to the castle and beyond.

Ber Street Gate was one of the first gates in the city to be built and was important because the road led directly from the south to the castle. The original gate was portcullised and the towers housed ordnance stores: it was equipped by Richard Spynk. A small section of the Ber Street wall and the angle where it turns into Queen's Road now stands behind iron grilles with a padlocked gate. Once the gate was furnished with a brass door, but a large part of the wall fell down killing four cows which were in an outhouse.

Near the other end of Queen's Road is the street called All Saint's Green. Here is the site of Brazen Gate, originally a tower with brass posterns which gave their name to the gate. This gate faced the country and Harford Bridge.*

---

*With the building of the railway bridge this became known as Harford Bridges.

When the doors were replaced by a single larger one the gate became known as the Iron Door. Being near the swine market, it was also called Swinemarket Gate.

The next section of remaining city wall is at the top of St Stephen's. Here a tower of particular interest may be seen to its best advantage from the top of a multi-storey car park behind it. This shows the brick vaulting which supported the first floor and the two fourteenth century gunports. A second piece of wall stands beside the steps by the underpass as the roundabout.

St Stephen's was a gate of tremendous size. First known as Nedham or Nedeham Gate, the origin of which is not known, it later took the parish name. One of the principal city gates, a lofty embattled tower, stood on either side, square on the city side, rounded outside. The west tower had a postern used as a footpath for pedestrians and the whole was embattled and enlightened with embrasures.

During Kett's Rebellion in 1549 the gate was battered down and the Earl of Warwick's soldiers entered the city. In 1561 a gibbet was erected in the Town Close immediately outside St Stephen's Gate.

The most important part of the city wall stands beside Chapel Field just beyond St Stephen's Gate. On the new Inner Ring Road the wall remains here are fully exposed and in some places stand only two feet from the edge of the road. The wall has been carefully repaired to show the original arrow slits, and the mural towers made safe, but with the close proximity of heavy traffic one wonders how much longer the wall will stand.

The next tower was formerly incorporated into the old Drill Hall and stood at St Giles' roundabout. Pulled down some years ago its memory is

The mural tower at St Stephen's roundabout. The remains seen from the top of a multi-storied car park.

The Black Tower at Norwich with its adjacent recessed loophole arches and the wall walk above.

...w Tower seen beside the river from Bishop's Gate direction at Norwich.

preserved by someone with imagination, for across the centre of the roundabout over the green sward, a double concrete line is filled in with rounded flints, to mark the curve of the wall, and a half-circle marks the mural tower.

The next gate was St Giles' which in 1288 was called Port St. Egidii. Like many other city gates St Giles' or Newport Gate had it leper house outside, with a master who prior to the Dissolution had religious duties. From St Giles' Gate the road dips down Grapes Hill and a line of flints marks the line of wall as far as St Benedict's Gate.

St Benedict's, or Westwick Gate, stood at the junction of St Benedict's and Dereham Road. During the fourteenth century Porta de Westwyck was an imposing embattled edifice with a lofty barbican or watch tower beside the gate. From here a watchman could see across the sheep walk and pasture lands at the edge of the Wensum. It was from this gate that pilgrims walked across the fields to the Shrine at Walsingham. This gate too had its contrasts — pilgrims behind a processional cross, and decapitated heads on top of poles, the dead from the gallows outside the gate.

On the far side of St Benedict's Gate a very interesting section of wall stands beside the footpath and the main road. Huge chunks of masonry with the original arched recesses broken through showing the thickness, the width and height of the arches.

At the bottom on the hill, at the junction of Westwick and Heigham Roads, stood Heigham Gate. Known as Hell Gate, it was built in a very poor quarter of Norwich, surrounded by marshy swamps and poor dwellings, a hellish place to live. Heigham Gate was a postern capable of admitting only low loads and small carts. No sign of this gate or the wall beyond exists today, and although it is known that the wall continued to the river's edge, the exact place is not known.

Beyond where this wall ends the river took over the defence of the town as far as the wall, over the river, next to St Martin's Gate.

This gate was also in a swampy, marshy area and poor part of Norwich. St Martin's at Oak Gate was named for an oak which once grew in St Martin's churchyard. Known also as Coslany Gate, meaning cow's long island, the area still answers to that name. A mural tower stands not far from the river's edge and beside it, in the basement of a derelict pub, is a huge piece of the original wall but no sign of the gate itself exists. Beyond the site of the gate, setts of flint mark the former wall for several hundred yards, and another section of very badly repaired mason ts he landscape, except for a beautiful cruciform arrowslit.

St Augustine's Gate, next in e enciente, was a battlemented brick edifice built as an entry to St Augustine's Street. This gate saw much of the troubles between the King and Parliament in 1642, but also saw the joys and excitement of the people at Justing Acre, an area just inside the wall where much festivity and jollity took place.

In the basement of, at the time of writing, a refrigerator shop is the lower half of one of the St Augustine Gate towers, on St Augustine's Street. Behind the shop, in Esdelle Street, is the tower itself with arcaded walling.

Houses hide wall remains if there are any, along Magpie Road as far as Magdalen Gate where the next part of the wall stands in all its ugliness. Originally known as Fyebrigge Gate because it led to Fye Bridge, Magdalen Gate had a leper house outside. Here there was a chapel for worship but no graveyard as all lepers were buried in All Saint's churchyard. The gate is known to have been built in 1339. Still known today as Magdalen Gate the gate has long since gone but, by the traffic lights, is the badly repaired section of wall. There were many battles here in the time of Kett's Rebellion and a gallows outside which saw many a man hanged, but like all the other gates it had a visually picturesque appearance.

At the Silver Road end of Bull Close Road, the next section of walling stands to a height of some three feet with the remains of recessed arches in good repair. At the far end of this wall is the most interesting tower of the Norwich enciente.

This is Pockthorpe Tower, a polygonal brick tower refaced in the nineteenth century. The ribbed vaulting is a special feature of medieval Norwich and remains today. From this tower the wall was right-angled to join onto the former Pockthorpe Gate a few hundred yards distant.

Pockthorpe Gate saw many troubles and was burnt more than once during Kett's Rebellion. The rebel army had a huge camp of 20,000 men on Mousehold Heath, many of whom swept down that hill to enter the city by Magdalen Gate, Pockthorpe Gate, by the river near Cow Tower and at Bishop's Gate. Beside the site of this gate is a printing works inside whose grounds is another part of the city wall, leading down to the River Wensum. This was the last section of the wall in the northern part of the defence.

On the opposite side of the river, a short distance away where the river bends south, the red brick Cow Tower stands on a stone plinth. This was formerly a toll house where the Prior of Norwich had men collecting money from vessels passing down river into Norwich. Later the tower became a prison and then part of the city defences. It is said to be one of the oldest brick structures in the country.

To quote from the journeys of Celia Fiennes,* in the seventeenth century, on Norwich, is a delight. "Norwich opens to view a mile distance by the help of a hill whereon is a little village...Then you proceed to the Citty which is walled

*Through England on a side saddle in the time of William and Mary. Celia Fiennes 1695-97.

Detail from a photograph of a coloured bas-relief of the old St Stephen's Gate. This bas-relief is high up on the wall of a nearby public house.

Bishop's Gate Bridge, Norwich, showing the bridge parapet with the semi-circular section where a turret to the gatehouse once stood.

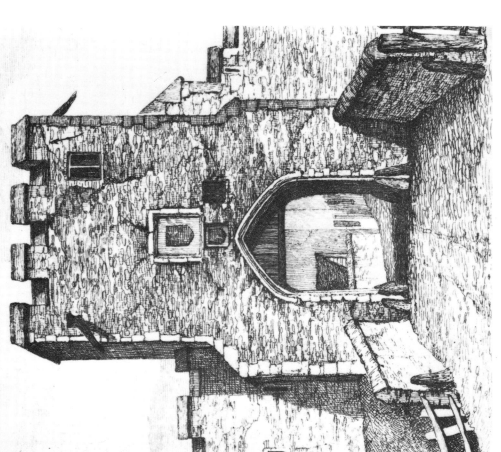

An engraving by Henry Ninham, 1864, from the 1720 drawing by John Kirkpatrick, showing the outside of St Martin's Gate, Norwich.
Norwich Central Library, Record Office.

round full of towers, except on the river side which serves for the wall;they seem in the best repaire of any walled citty I know...I enter'd the West gate*...a great Well house with a wheele to wind up the water for the good of the publicke...this brings you into a broad space called the Hay market which is on a hill, a very steep descent all well pitch'd,this comes to another space for a market to sell hoggs in...On the Castle hill you see the whole Citty at once... The town is a mile and a halfe from the North to the South gate, just by one of the Churches there is a wall made of flints that are headed very finely and cut so exactly square and even, to shutt in one to another, that the whole wall is made without cement at all they say, but it appears to be very little if any mortar, it looks well very smooth shineing and black."

Bishop's Gate further down the river was built on an existing bridge in 1295, and so called because it led to the Palace of the Bishop. This was not an entrance or an exit in the city wall but a tower with gates protecting a bridge and the roads leading to and from that bridge. Bishopgate was one of the principal gateways into Norwich from the east and of major importance in the defence of Norwich. Kett's men swarmed across the bridge; it was the entry point of the Black Death; and scene of the executions at the nearby Lollard's Pit.

Pull's Ferry, south of Bishop's Bridge, was, in its earliest days, known as Sandling's Ferry. This was a water gate which prevented unwanted entry to the cathedral. Originally a small navigable channel beneath the water gate led to the cathedral and this stretch of water was used to convey Caen stone to the site when the cathedral was built. It seems logical that Pull's Ferry would play some defensive part in the history of Norwich although the gate was not built for such purposes. It is mentioned here because it is essential that devotees of city walls should know its true purpose.

Recently a riverside walk has been laid out making it possible to see parts of the river which were a section of the city's water defence. This walk leads from Foundry Bridge near Thorpe Station, along past Pull's Ferry and Bishop's Bridge, as far as Cow Tower, following the line of the river from the Yachting Station, past a crinkle-crankle wall, thence to the riverside. From Foundry Bridge in the opposite direction one may walk via existing paths beside the river, past old timber and grain warehouses;past the ship turning point in the river; and commercial shipping anchored there; to the swing bridge beside the old Boom Towers. This completes the circuit of the unique defences of the City of Norwich, indeed a fine City.

There have been suggestions that the artificial hill of the castle mound is a burial mound. The castle stands atop, serene on its grassy, and in the spring, flower-decked mound, seemingly aware that it is unlikely that further "digs", to prove or disprove such suggestions, will ever be permitted. Here whatever is unknown of history and prehistory can remain asleep.

*St Benedict's Gate.

Caistor St Edmunds

The Iceni, inhabitants of part of East Anglia, formed a league to fight against Roman oppression. They were defeated and Boadicea was flogged, the aristocracy was reduced to slavery and the settlements reduced to ashes. They had reason not to accept the defeat.

John Speed's *Theatre of the Empire of Great Britaine, 1611,* says, "Prasutagus and Boduo (Boadicea), King and Queene of the Icenians, a people unshaked by war, and themselves rich; the only cause of their ruines, for which the Romans then warred; were brought to destruction upon this insuing occasion. King Prasutagus dying, (in AD 60), by will left Nero his heire (supposing by this means to leave his state the safer), together with the protection of his two daughters. These, contrary to trust, were abused and defloured, the mother Boduo turned out of all, and against all manly civilitie, or womanhood respect, contumeiously and despitefully whipped. In revenge of which unsufferable wrongs shee so oppressed the Romans, that at one battell seventy thousand of these slaughtered bodies, shee sacrificed to her dead husband's Ghost; and hath left the fame of her proceedings registered, even by her enemies themselves, to her immortall and never dying memory. The strong Cities, Camulodunum, and Verolanium, she sacked with the rage of merciless warre; Petilius, Lieutenant of the ninth Legion, she discomfited, Catus the Procurator she drove over the seas, Posthumus the Camps-master durst not resist her, all indeed feared the valour of this heroicke Lady, whose lawes were not martiall to save upon ransome; whose revenge was not pacified with yieldings or submission, nor did she thinke there was blood enough in the Romans to imbrue the altars of her assisting gods, or to wash off the staine of ignoble and unmanly injuries. But when sucesse altered, after losse, and valourous resitance, shee made an end of her life by poyson, lest living she should see either her owne miseries in their triumphs, or leave her remem-rance in the records of their lavish or selfe-pleasing historians. Her Coyne of gold we have here expressed, the forme shield-like, and upon the embossement thus inscribed: Boduo."

After the rebellion which must have wiped out a generation of men, the Romans did not appear to impose a military occupation at Venta Icenorum for any length of time although the Iceni were unable then to govern themselves. It is thought that Roman forts in the area controlled the people by isolating them. This was of great importance to the tribe and no doubt to the Romans, and held back any development of Venta for many generations. In fact it was not until some eighty years after the death of Prasutagus that the early huts and timber houses of the town were replaced by stone buildings.

A civitas capital was established at Venta Icenorum, now Caistor St Edmunds, where local government could be administered, according to the usual pattern of the Roman Empire over the tribal lands of the Iceni. Why

This photograph of Caistor St Edmunds shows the whole layout of Roman Street, sites of the main compass points gates are clearly visible. Aerial photography by Dr. J. K. St Joseph, *Cambridge University*

Caistor was chosen as the capital is unknown. Many historians believed Norwich to be the site of Venta Icenorum.

The ancient town of Caistor St Edmunds, also known as Caistor-by-Norwich, is situated near the confluence of the rivers Yare and Wensum. Known as Venta Icenorum it was walled soon after 200 A.D., an area of about 45 acres were enclosed. Two-thirds of the population lived outside these walls, and there are still many visible signs of where roads led to the outlying countryside and the trade routes of Britain.

The walls are thought to have been built on top of earlier defences, because of the double ditch running along beside the south "wall". During Roman occupation there was a ditch 80 to 100 feet wide with timber bridges leading to the gates. The town wall was 20 feet high and some 11 feet thick with several bastions. Much of the town has been excavated but now lies buried under cultivation. Legend says the city was part of Boadicea's capital, but there is no proof of this. The present church of Caistor St Edmunds stands inside the walls of the ancient town and is largely built of Roman materials taken from the old walls.

Aerial photographs show the network of streets at Caistor, both inside the walls and outside to the north, south and east sides. To the north-east outside the walls streets radiate outwards. Here coins and early pottery have been found indicating that this was the earliest section of the town. The main streets within the walls are said to be dated c. A.D. 70. The number of streets outside the walls indicate that the early town was much larger than the area which was finally walled soon after A.D.200. Even today from a high vantage point on the main road (A140), the street plan may be seen in the enclosed, now cultivated area. The banks and ditches are quite clearly visible to anyone on foot. Standing well back from the banks and remains of the walls, the north, south, east and west gateway gaps are visible, marked by the dips in the banks.

A sewerage system existed and possibly an aqueduct, though the latter has not been found. The walls enclosed baths with frigidarium and tepidarium, dressing rooms and latrines; a market place; a forum; a piazza some 100 feet square with flights of steps leading up to a basilica; offices; three Romano-Celtic temples; and houses. A small bust of Geta found near Caistor Hall was said to be an emperor or possibly a god; a Roman mirror; a figure of Bacchus; a terra-cotta relief of a head of Diana; a figure of Mercury decorating a bronze saucepan handle, found near the East Gate, are among the many and varied finds of this interesting and important site.

Despite the many finds at Venta nothing is known of the personal inhabitants of the town, for no inscription has been found, except for the name P. Anicus Sedatus carved on a stone occultist's stamp—which in fact tells us very little. Professor Donald Atkinson in his unpublished notes suggests that

Venta came finally to a violent end during a massacre, because of a cremation cemetery of some thirty five people including women and children, which he found east of the town. The skeletal remains had suffered violent blows with blunt instruments.

The north bank, outside, lies within the bounds of a turkey farm. Here the bank rises to some twenty to thirty feet in places, being much hidden by trees. Some sections of Roman wall may be seen, with Roman brick coursing, two lines of red bricks set among the flints and stones, behind the bushes, trees and weeds. Further along the north bank slopes gently down to marshy fields below.

Along the southern side the ground drops steeply some 20 feet to the fields. Looking west one sees the undulations were field meets "wall", each dip once a Roman road leading from the city to the outlying country. Steep banks and ditches mark the eastern side of the town.

The South Gate had an opening thirteen feet wide and the approach to the gate is still clearly visible from the A140 Ipswich Road. When this part of the wall was excavated door socket holes were found. It has been suggested that there was once a tower over the South Gate, like the one at Duncan's Gate at Colchester. Guard rooms were at either end of the tower and could be reached from the rampart inside the walls. Five bastions are known to have existed at Venta Icenorum.

The west bank remains are low in height, with a ruined Roman tower, hidden among trees part way along the length of the bank. It has treble bands of Roman brick coursing. As the banks are continuous, bridges were probably built to cross the ditches as no other access would have been possible.

Inside the field facing east, a line of grass shows. This is never cut with the harvester, for obviously a stony strip of ground lies underneath, where a

On the south bank at Caistor St Edmunds, looking west, the ground drops steeply some twenty feet to the fields outside, each dip a Roman road leading to the outlying countryside.

former road once lay. Even when the cows have grazed for a considerable time this line remains firmly drawn across the field. All round inside the field there are signs that the former walls were reveted with earth both inside and out.

This 45 acre field is important historically, and as part of our heritage, should in no way be destroyed. The drowsy farm atmosphere, with grazing cows, marshy river-side surround, wild flowers, weeds and cloud blown sky, must not let us forget what has gone before, nor what lies beneath the plough. Here is a Roman site, so near to Norwich, which should be laid out in permanent excavated glory for all to see — perhaps another Fishbourne awaits us here.

Ptolemy (Claudius Ptolemaeus), native of Egypt, mathematician, astronomer and geographer (A.D. 127-151), charted much of the world in his geographia, often in an imperfect and vague manner. He knew much of the British coastline but put Ireland further north than Wales — twisted Scotland round to the west, placing Northern Ireland and Britain on the same parallel. BUT he called Venta Icenorum the one noteworthy town of the Iceni, and placed it at the end of a route from London by Colchester to Caistor-by-Norwich. If this was the one town of the Iceni, then Boadicea certainly walked here.

*   *   *   *   *

New Buckenham

Before the Norman Conquest Buckenham was owned by Ralf Guader, Earl of Norfolk, and a son of Edward the Confessor's Master of the Horse. A wealthy man in his own right, he had inherited his mother's estates in Brittany. Before the Conquest, he owned the two Buckenham parishes, St Andrew's and All Saints, for New Buckenham did not then exist. Having quarrelled with the Earl of East Anglia who seized his property, he went into exile, returning in 1066 with William the Conqueror at the Battle of Hastings. For his services at Hastings he was given back his lands. Ralf married the sister of Roger, Earl of Hereford against the wishes of the Norman King. A revolt followed and Ralf Guader was beaten in battle by Odo, Bishop of Bayeux, the Conqueror's half-brother. Ralf returned to live in Brittany and his estates were once more confiscated. The estates were then given by William to his follower William D'Albini, who had also fought with him at Hastings. D'Albini was an ancestor of the Earls of Arundel and Sussex, and of the Mowbrays. It is D'Albini who abandoned his castle at Old Buckenham to build one at New Buckenham.

Blomefield tells the legend of how D'Albini's son, another William, earned the sobriquet, William the Strong Hand. Apparently while young William was in France he was commanded to attend a tournament by the widowed Queen of France. The prize for the victor was the queen's hand in marriage. Young D'Albini won but he was already betrothed to Adelicia, the widow of Henry I of England. The French Queen was jealous and angry, so planned to have him killed by a lion in her garden. In those days it was a status symbol to have wild animals chained in the grounds. The legend states that William pushed his arm into the lion's mouth and tore out its tongue, thus earning the name by which he became known. On return to England in 1138 he married Queen Adelicia, and was granted a coat of arms of the figure of a tongueless lion. On his marriage to Adelicia he was given Arundel castle and the Earldom thereof, as his wife's dowry. This very rich and self-important man died in 1176.

The D'Albinis are buried at Wymondham, the abbey itself being founded by the first D'Albini early in the twelfth century as the Priory Church. Unfortunately no D'Albini tomb remains at Wymondham Abbey today. It is thought that the first D'Albini, who died in 1155, was buried in the Priory Church before the original high altar where his wife, Maud the daughter of Sir Roger Bigod, and their child had previously been buried. Two coffins containing the bodies of a woman and a prematurely born child were unearthed in 1834 in the churchyard and these bodies seem to be those of Maud and her child. William the Strong Hand's son, yet another William, Earl of Arundel, was one of the Magna Carta witnesses at Runnymede in 1215. Six years later he died near Rome while returning from a Crusade. His body was preserved in salt and he was later buried at Wymondham.

William the Strong Hand built a castle of earth and timber at Old Buckenham which had earthworks, a conical mound, cattle enclosures, banks and ditches. He soon thought, however, that the castle was too small, so had a larger new one built at New Buckenham under a charter granted in 1151 and the old one pulled down. The site of the old castle he gave to the Austin Canons, founding a Priory called Buckenham Abbey. The foundation deed of the Priory says that he gave the Canons eighty acres of land, *cum sede castelli et castellum diruendum*. By giving away the castle site he made sure that it could never again be used for defensive purposes. The new site was protected by a marshy stream and was near a minor Roman road.

An oval ditch and bank remains from the former Priory and earlier castle. Harrod believed that previously a Roman camp stood at that spot, but excavations have yet to prove him right.

When William's new castle was built at New Buckenham, it had no conical mound as architectural and layout ideas had changed. With the coming of the Normans the era of polygonal or square stone castles built upon flat ground had begun. Great earthworks went out of fashion and stonework came into its own. Earlier, towers had been square, but now it was realized that circular towers were more difficult for the enemy to scale and that

New Buckenham castle keep with walls some fifteen feet high and a low doorway entrance through the thick wall at ground level.

circular ones, because of the pure strength of the masonry in the inside curve, were less likely to fall under attack.

New Buckenham castle is a circular banked enclosure some 216 feet in diameter, with an oval outer bailey to the east. Inside this bank were buildings: a central keep, two circular towers and a gateway. A low circular tower built in part onto the inner side of the bank in the south east is of rubble and flint. The 11 foot thick walls are divided by a wall crossing it. This tower has no windows or staircase, and was probably merely a cellar approached by a ladder. It is part of the original structure of 1146. This is "probably the earliest circular keep in England, possibly in Europe."

In the centre of New Buckenham is the seventeenth century Market Cross, recently renovated, which has wooden Tuscan columns and a whipping post, said to be the last in Norfolk.

New Buckenham has been declared a Conservation Area, under the Civic Amenities Act of 1967 and while no medieval houses remain, the original grid pattern of the streets still exists. St Martin's perpendicular church has fine clerestory windows and the church with the Market Place and Cross remain features of the village.

Conservation of other walls, buildings and landscape areas are under discussion and the castle, which stands beyond the village at the western end, will be preserved. The keep, while massive, is relatively uninteresting. The walls are fifteen feet high with putlog holes, for scaffolding, in a regular pattern indicating accuracy and level in building. A low doorway through the thick wall and an arch ten feet high leads through the central dividing wall. Holes at ground level have an unknown purpose and are blocked up outside. Because of the width of the interior, 48 feet across, the floor above would have been supported on the cross wall, and the present entrance would not have been there when the keep was built. Entrance was on the first floor by an outside wooden staircase, because ground floor entry would provide an easy access to an enemy.

A grassy path leads round the outside of a hidden moat, to an iron grille gate with a padlock which protects the castle entrance, made in the thirteenth century. Inside the gate the grassy path lies on top of part of a stone bridge. Wooden planks lie across the way, chained together and fixed in place with horseshoe-shaped clips, at the site of the former drawbridge. Beautiful old trees stand beside the edges of the banks which enclose the inner bailey and keep. Here the gatehouse would have stood, a rectangular tower with a chamber above its entrance. A circular tower is thought to have stood on either side of the gatehouse. Huge chunks of masonry lie lop-sided against the edge of the bank. The moat has banks covered with grasses and weeds, whilst wind ripples the water in the moat.

The circular bailey wall, an earthen bank, is also grass covered. A tangled path follows the top of this ring and one may walk right round the bank with glimpses between the encircling trees of the village beneath, the church, and houses, the farm and St Mary's chapel.

During the fourteenth century the entrance to the castle was from the east side of the inner bailey and archaeologists give evidence that at that period the waters of the moat were undermining the rampart entrance. For greater safety and to prevent any more of the castle subsiding into the ditch, the height of the rampart was raised. In the process the gatehouse was covered over and the keep half buried. This did not matter as by the fourteenth century it was used only for storage. A new gatehouse was built at the western side of the inner bailey, the entrance that exists today. A new oval outer bailey was built to protect it and the old barbican bailey in the east fell into disuse.

The horseshoe barbican bailey is still marked by ditch and bank marks, though not by name, on present Ordnance Survey maps. The fourteenth century south and western outer bailey however is not shown which means it was long since levelled. The line of the modern road does however give an idea of its southern limits, and St Mary's chapel is still marked on maps.

An attempt to seize the castle for the king in 1461 was made because Sir John Knyvet, the owner, failed to pay the £100 owing to the king for his barony. A report on the siege says, "we entered the outer Ward of the Castle to the footbridge, called a draght brigge, across the water and found it raised so that we could not enter. Alice, wife of John, appeared at the tower over the inner foot of the bridge, keeping the Castle with slings, plaveises, faggots, timber and other armaments of war. 'Master Twyer', she cried, 'ye be a justice (Escheator) of the pees and I require your to keep the pees for I wall not leve the possess of this castle to dye there fore, and if ye begyn to breake the pees or make any warre to gete the place of me, I shall defend me, for liefer I had in such wyse to dye an to be slayne when my husband cometh home, for he chargeth me to keep it.'" The besiegers retired before this threat!

New Buckenham castle was certainly inhabited until the mid-seventeenth century, as a will, probably of a servant, dated 20th March shows. "I, Edward Yelverton, of Carlton Rode, bequeath to My ladie Ursula Yelverton, wife of Sir William Yelverton, Baronet, one steel mill, now in the granary at Buckenham, Castle, and to my loving cousin, Roger Woodhouse, a picture now hanging in my chamber at Buckenham Castle."

After the generations of D'Albini ownership the castle passed to the female heirs, the Tatteshalls, Cliftons and Knyvets. Later the castle came into other hands by inheritance or purchase. Sir Philip Knyvet inherited the castle in 1594, together with its lands. In 1649 he had the castle pulled down and sold the estate to Hugh Audley for 18,508 pounds and 10 pence.

While no tombs or tablets exist to remember the D'Albinis, there are other reminders of New Buckenham castle within the nave of the great Abbey church at Wymondham. A corbel with the Arms of Sir John Clifton has its place high up in the nave just below the lovely hammerbeam roof. This may be found on the right of the nave immediately above the pulpit.

The Chapel of St Mary, now a barn on the road south of the castle, is Norman, built for retainers of the castle. The eastern end had an apse, and the western end an original bell cot, later altered to become a chimney. Blomefield says it was used by a custos and two or three chaplains, his brethren who dwelt in the west end of it. This was the only place of worship in the burh of New Buckenham, until the present church was built.

The castle, held for seven hundred years by many illustrious families, was the scene of many stirring events all of which have now faded into history.

North along Church Street at its end is a field which is part burial ground. At right angles to the road here a grassy track runs beside the buildings which were once farm buildings. Now stables, they stand behind a high brick wall of a private house. Outside and at the foot of the walls lies the remains of the moat or a Town Ditch. The corner buildings are built over part of this moat.

Further along the dry moat one sees St Martin's church tower over the high brick. Just beyond this point a vehicle and foot bridge leads across the moat, only a few feet wide into the grounds of the house. The moat continues beside the wall, with tree stumps on its bank, then curves and widens and indeed actually has a few inches of water where trees overhang it beside New Buckenham Common. Here at right angles the moat, much narrower, cuts across the common to be lost at the edge of the B1113, the road to Norwich. It seems that this Town Ditch would have connected the castle enclosure moat in former times. If not, then the Town Ditch would provide no protection for the townspeople which was its purpose. However archaeologists have yet to excavate New Buckenham Town Ditch.

A gold ring exists in the Norwich Castle Museum, found at the site of Old Buckenham castle, in 1860, bearing the inscription: NUNS QUAN DYN PLERA — Whenever God pleases. This ring may have belonged to Maud or the original William D'Albini.

Another relic of New Buckenham castle, now in Dereham church, is an old oak chest which stands near a former side chapel and was once used as an altar. In 1976 it was restored, when a new lid and base replaced the deteriorated originals. Fortunately the main beauties of the chest, intricately carved, front and sides and the lock, remained in excellent condition.

The town moat at New Buckenham with the foot and vehicle bridge leading to the grounds of a private house.

The lock is of decorative iron tracery with a clasp in the form of a three dimensional lantern-type bell turret. At each end of the chest three ladies stand in medieval costume holding ecclesiastical symbols. On one end the three women hold a broken rod or staff, an entwined circlet and a mirror, and on the other the women hold a cross of Jesus Christ, a heart and a scourge. The front of the chest is also decorated with six medieval ladies and a central theme. From left to right they hold the sword and scales, pincers for pulling the nails out of Christ on the cross, a church, a cross, a heart and a round tower-like edifice with a snake-monster emerging from the doorway. A Latin Bestiary of the twelfth century mentions snakes as having three odd things about them. First when the skin grows old snakes go into a tight crack in the rocks laying aside the old skin by scraping it off. This symbolizes the spiritual Rock, Jesus, and the tight crack, the Strait Gate. Secondly, a snake when drinking first spews out its poison into a hole, as we, in church, when hearing the heavenly word ought to cast out bad and earthly longings. The third concerns Adam's nakedness in Paradise when the Serpent was not able to spring upon him. When man dressed in mortality the serpent did spring. Here the Serpent (and Man) is passing through the crack in the Rock (the Church), and cleansing himself. All this in a carving of a church-serpent no more than three inches high.

The central theme is of pure delight, being in two parts. The upper part is semi-circular, having two medieval page boys, one kneeling, the other on one knee, both holding a bell-rope, or door-handle. They appear to be on top of a

Bridge over castle moat, New Buckenham.

church (of Christ), so perhaps are in heaven. Beneath is a nativity: Mary and Joseph and the Christ-child are in medieval costume, with ox and ass behind, and an angel in medieval costume above.

This is an early seventeenth century chest having an oval brass inscription plate on the lid. A lion passant above a crown surmounts a simple shield with points sinister. Beneath the scroll with motto: KNOW YOURSELF BE GOOD:

As a Token of Respect Towards his Native Place
Samuel Rash Esq.
On the I Day of Jan 1786 Presented to the church of East Dereham.
THIS CHEST
For the purpose of Keeping together and Preserving the Deeds
Records and other Writings belonging to the Parish.
Tradition says this Curious Chest (and Lock)
is upwards of Four Hundred Years Old Taken out
of the Ruins of Buckenham Castle and many years since
the Property of the Noble Family of the Former Dukes of Norfolk
and supposed to be used by them for
Depositing their Money and Other Valuables.

This chest alone tells of the glories of those past days, of the skill and craftsmanship which went into its carving. What other relics of far off days may come to light when the New Buckenham Town Ditch is excavated, we cannot know.

4. Heart of East Anglia

THETFORD — FRAMLINGHAM — BURY ST EDMUNDS

Thetford

MANY miles of dense forest still cover a vast area of the heart of East Anglia. Thetford stands but a short distance from this forest, beside the Icknield Way, with, to the east, the line of the Peddars Way running north to south only two miles distant. A Roman road to the east of the town led to New Buckenham and thence to a junction with Pye Road, the important Roman road which led from Colchester in the South to Caistor St Edmunds in the north, to Kirby Bedon and then possibly on to Caister-next-Yarmouth, also known as Caister-on-Sea, the Roman commercial seaport.

Thetford is ancient in the extreme. According to Martin, "Sitomagus continued to be a fenced and royal city from the unfortunate overthrow of Boadicea until the establishment of the Heptarchy, and was known to Antonius Ptolemy, by this name, when Norwich, Lynn and Yarmouth were yet in infancy." Anciently called Theodford it was formerly a place of great importance, the metropolis of East Anglia and a residence of her kings. Originally a town of the ancient Britons, then a Roman station, Thetford in our time is a small growing market town, with considerable London overspill growth. Camden says that Sitomagus is derived from Sit, or Thet, the name of a tributary of the Little Ouse which runs through the town, and Magus, which as Pliny says, signifies a city.

It was called by the Romans the city upon the river Sit or Thet; and corruptly Simomagus and Sinomagus, on Roman Empire maps.

At the eastern end of the town there are extensive remains of fortifications. A large artificial mound with lofty banks and ditches, the latter said possibly to be the work of the early Kings of East Anglia, perhaps the work of the Iceni. East of the mound is a large area 300 feet square, evidently intended and indeed quite adequate for a parade of troops employed in defence. The mound is 100 feet high, and approximately 1,000 feet in circumference at base. The remaining ramparts are some 20 feet high and the fossa from 60 to 70 feet wide.

The mound called Castle Hill is said to be in the Celtic style of fortification and characteristic of those found in Celtic countries, but never in Roman, Saxon or Danish. Archaeological facts seem indisputable that the Romans, Saxons, and Danes found the great fortifications on their arrival and because they understood its importance as a means of defence, took advantage and occupied the city. It is impossible to fix a date for the erection of the mound, although the late Saxons are known to have built a town ditch to defend Thetford. The mound however is more likely to be of a much earlier date.

This earthwork was a right-angled parallelogram with the corners rounded off. From east to west was the longest length and there were two ramparts with each ditch defended. Parallel to the west side the steep mount, or keep, rises, surrounded completely by a ditch. The sides slope steeply forming an angle of about 40 degrees from the horizontal. There is no known path to the summit, although a rough track shows today where countless children have clambered up. The chief entrance to Castle Hill was from the north through the second or inner rampart. A motte and bailey castle was built on top of the mound subsequent to the Norman Conquest but was demolished in 1173. William de Warenne, who married Gundreda, the Conqueror's daughter, was Lord of Thetford Castle so there must have been a castle there at that period.

One writer suggests that "the key to the mystery of Thetford Mound is not to be found in East Anglia but in far away Wiltshire, within the orbit of Avebury, Silbury Hill and Stonehenge, all products of the Mesolithic Age, about four thousand years ago."* Silbury Hill, the largest artificial mound in Europe, was always considered to be a Bronze Age barrow, and an extraordinarily large one. Various excavations of the hill have taken place. A vertical tunnel dug from the top of the hill, down through the centre to the original ground level, revealed no form of burial. During the nineteenth century a horizontal tunnel also failed to find human remains. During 1968-9, BBC 2 sponsored a dig under the expertise of Professor R. J. C. Atkinson who had excavated Stonehenge. He headed a team of miners, zoologists, geographers and geologists, but still no bones were found. By radio carbon dating it was proved conclusively that the whole of Silbury Hill was thrown up circa 2260 B.C., four thousand five hundred years ago. This places it in the latter half of the Stone Age of simple farmers. Silbury Hill is 130 feet high, Thetford 80 feet, with a perimeter of about 1,375 feet, Silbury Hill 1,000 feet. Might there not indeed be an affinity between the two mounds? Will Thetford mound ever

Dim Corridors by R. B. Clover, Modern Press 1948.

The mound at Thetford, called Castle Hill, showing the rough track where countless children have clambered to the summit.

Studio Five, Thetford.

be excavated to the same extent as Silbury and its real origin be discovered? Stone Age man lived close to nature, was one with nature, understood nature and realized nature's true significance in the universe. They worshipped the Great Mother Goddess, who was responsible for birth, marriage and death. Professor Atkinson's theory is that to men of that age pregnant, huge squatting mounds, were hills giving birth to nature.

They threw up Silbury Hill as a magnificent replica of the divine Goddess, for they saw all the universe in human female form. The ground plan of Silbury Hill and lakes, the ditches surrounding the hill fill with water at certain times of the year, shows the neck and breasts of the goddess, her knees and full belly. All the Neolithic people were doing was to emphasise and enlarge the truths they knew, and build this truth over large for all to see. Perhaps the origin of Thetford mound, lost in antiquity, holds some new, and ancient lost truth.

The perimeter of the mound today looks wild and uncared for, with its ditches littered with rubbish. The mound itself is green and bare of trees except for two which grow on the top, as they did in an engraving of 1821. In its day the mound ensured that its owners had command over the Icknield Way where it crosses the Thet and the Little Ouse. At that time the land was ill-drained with ugly primeval forest. Still the mound rises from its surround of deep dry moats, run between the remains of a double wall.

William de Warenne's castle would not have been the same castle used by the Romans. His was on Thetford mound, theirs was Red Castle, further to the west beyond the London Road (A11).

The town in Ethelred's time was situated then as now, on both sides of the river which was wider, and at high water could be forded by large blocks of stone placed across it. During this time the meadows between Red Castle and the river were still under water and also Devil's Ditch or Town Ditch, by the Nunnery. The southern fosse and ramparts of the Castle Hill were in perfect state and the space between them and the Thet was narrow and marshy so no houses were built there.

Twenty thousand Danes landed in the broads of East Anglia in the late summer of 865 and wintered outside Thetford. Edmund was unable to engage so large an army as he only had local levies. He used his available force as resistance fighters of which he proved himself a very able leader.

In October, 866, having mounted and trained their cavalry and stolen the harvest, the Danes moved out to fulfill their intended task, the conquest of Northumbria; Hingwar, Ubba and Alfdene were among their commanders. York fell in November 867 and, having subdued Northumbria, they decided to attack Mercia and captured Nottingham. Burrhed, King of Mercia, appealed to his brother-in-law, Ethelred of Wessex, who appeared with a large army and his brother, Alfred, and they were joined by Edmund of East Anglia. The Danes, seeing these reinforcements, retired to York where they spent the following year.

Edmund was not slow in building an army and appears to have used the Danes' long stay in York for the purpose. In 869 Hingwar reappeared in East Anglia with the land force near Newmarket and Ubba came with supplies by water to sack Ely and Soham. The Danes having outflanked or being about to outflank Devils Dyke, the most obvious defensive point, Edmund decided to make his stand at the other crossing point, Thetford. Hingwar followed and an all out battle with terrific carnage ensued. Edmund appears to have had the best of the battle as he was left in possession of the battlefield and buried his own and, most unusual, the enemy dead. Even today stories are told of children refusing to pick blackberries or collect fir cones on a mound at Thetford because they "belong to Edmund's men". Ubba arrived from Soham with reinforcements and Edmund, unable to face this new force, retired. Bryan Houghton, accepted by most as the foremost living authority on St Edmund, has carefully considered the theories about where Edmund died after the battle at Thetford. He rejects the most commonly held and slightly romantic story of his capture and martyrdom at Hoxne, Sutton or the South Lopham tower and he settles for Hellesdon, near Norwich. The death of Edmund on 20th November 869, the manner of his death, the wolf guarding his severed head and the like are not in dispute. Unfortunately we do not know the exact date of the battle. The East Anglian king who was crowned at Bures on Christmas Day, 855, a king, martyr and patron saint of England before St George, enters the history of Thetford whose inhabitants must have known him well.

In 1004 Sweyn invaded East Anglia and burnt Thetford with several other places. In 1010 with the total defeat of Ulfketel, the Saxon earl, the town suffered severely. So if the square beside the mound was a parade ground, no doubt it was involved in training troops for the many battles of Thetford.

Thetford, The Heart of East Anglia, has a tiny market and a small museum, the usual shops of a small town, a new library and ample car parks. There are magnificent Priory ruins on the outskirts of the town and still many interesting old houses remain. But the main delight to me in Thetford is the huge mound to the north. Quiet, remote, grassy-green, mysterious, enormous. What does it really mean?

* * * * *

Framlingham

The small market town of Framlingham lies about thirty miles away from the central East Anglian towns of Thetford and Bury St Edmunds. Placed almost on the Roman road which originally swept from Dunwich across the land to meet the main Roman road from Colchester to Godmanchester, the Via Devana, today it has diminished in importance.

In Domesday Book called Franchincham, otherwise known as Freynlingham or Friendling, meaning stranger (referring to the Danes) and ham, (a place or dwelling, boro or village), or from Fromus the name of the river. Names ending in ham, ing, or ingham are usually known to belong to the earliest Anglo-Saxon place-name in England - Framlingham - of the Framingas.

Framlingham is built on a high bluff above the mere, and the river running through the town was a natural defence. Because of this it is thought that Framlingham was a fortified town from early times. First the Saxons and afterwards the Danes held it. However there is no known evidence of early fortification, nor of a motte and bailey castle as was usual shortly after the Norman Conquest.

An archaeological report of 1954 recorded a seventh century Anglian settlement with a wooden stockade on the site of the present bowling green, which lies over a burial ground, and the meadow beside the castle.

The first buildings of the castle in 1100 and 1101 were those of a timber fortified dwelling-house, with defending ditches and palisades, not in any way intended for military use. The site of the manor and lands of Framlingham were given to Roger Bigod by Henry I. When Bigod's son William died in the White Ship (1120), in the same disaster which claimed the heir to the throne, the inheritance of Framlingham passed to the second son Hugh Bigod. Hugh was a strong supporter of King Stephen, who for his services created him Earl of Norfolk or the East Angles. He replaced the more important timber buildings with stone ones.

When King Stephen died Hugh entered the service of the new king, Henry II. Bigod proved treacherous. The king, to whom he had surrendered, ordered his fortification of Framlingham and other castles to be dismantled in 1174.

The building of Framlingham castle employed the then new techniques of using a curtain wall, interspersed with tall towers and a gate house.

Two and a half miles south east of Framlingham there is a charming village called Parham. Through this village, as indeed through Framlingham town itself, the river Ore flows, now almost unnoticed. But the river is said to

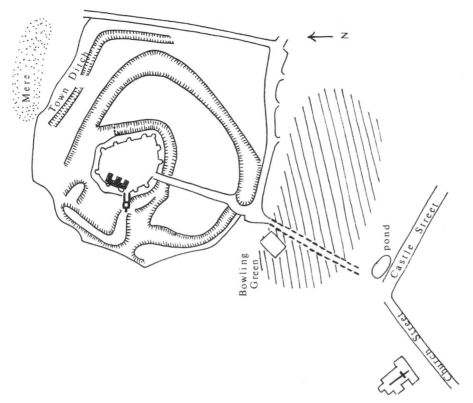

This plan shows castle, banks and ditches, Town Ditch, bowling green, mere, pond and, hatched, possible site of the early wooden stockade at Framlingham.

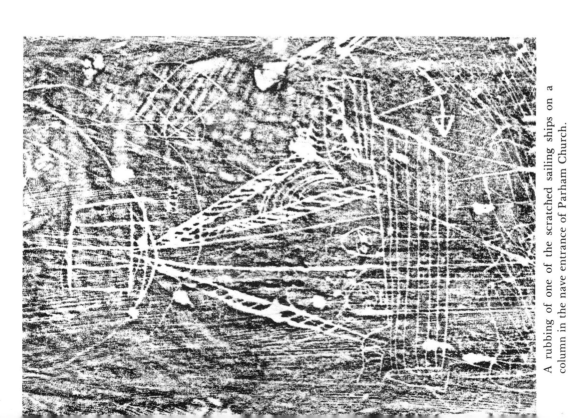

A rubbing of one of the scratched sailing ships on a column in the nave entrance of Parham Church.

have been navigable from the sea. Shipping would have been of great importance when the castle was built. It was built of Caen stone which was floated up the river from Normandy.

Framlingham castle is surrounded by two ditches. To the north and east there is also a third ditch which is always called, and marked on maps and plans, the Town Ditch. This third ditch commences from the mere on the north side of the castle, bearing the appellation of the tun or town ditch, which extended in an almost circular form along the east side of the town along the Back-Lane, at the bottom of which it emptied itself into the river near the bridge there. This ditch is believed to be the former limit of the borough on the east or land-side of the town, the river being its limit on all the other sides. The part of it which was immediately connected with the castle, and which intersects the castle lands, can be traced across the whole extent of a meadow, adjacent to the outer ditch and called the Black-Hill. Near the bottom of Back-Lane, it passed into what is now, but originally was not, a separate meadow, called the Paddock, lying within the park, where it discharged itself into the mere. Near the town the ditch is partly open and runs at the back of the dwellings on the west side of the upper part of the Back-Lane. The remaining part, which extends towards the river, is either built over or enclosed. Presumably this Town Ditch was cleaned and kept serviceable by the inhabitants either as volunteers or employees.

In 1178 when Hugh Bigod was crossing a ford at Framlingham on horseback, the horse stumbled and Hugh fell to his death on the point of his sword, thus meeting his death at the age of seventy-eight. Roger, his son, rebuilt the castle shortly afterwards. When King John stayed there in 1213 he saw how independent were the Bigods in their stronghold.

King John's foreign mercenaries besieged and captured the castle in the Civil War of 1215. When John died the estates were returned to the family. The fourth earl, Roger, Earl of Norfolk and Suffolk, was made Earl Marshal in 1246. At the death of the fifth earl, another Roger, the castle passed to the crown as he left no heir. In 1312 Thomas de Brotherton, half-brother of Edward II, was made Earl of Norfolk and Earl Marshal with all the estates and by marriage Framlingham passed into the hands of the Mowbrays and then to the Howards, the Dukes of Norfolk. Edward VI granted Framlingham to his sister, Mary, in May 1553 and she stayed there, her standard flying over the gatehouse tower. Surrounded by her supporters she remained at the castle until the succession was clear when she left for London to be crowned Queen.

It was not until 1636 when Sir Robert Howard died that the castle ceased to be lived in. Sir Robert bequeathed it to Pembroke College, Cambridge, providing the castle was dismantled, except for the stone buildings, the other

This aerial photograph of Framlingham castle shows the Town Ditch circling round from the left.   *Crown Copyright*

materials were used for building alms houses and a school for 40 poor boys. The poor house was built on the site of the Great Hall and remained in use until 1837 when it became a county court. Repeatedly history states, "the king visited the castle"; this happened throughout the many reigns, so Framlingham saw much pomp and ceremony.

At last in 1913, the castle passed to the Commissioners of Works as an ancient monument. Because Framlingham was not involved in the Civil War, the battlements are very well preserved and remain as part of the glory of the castle.

Now the town is quiet, clean and neat, with market place, small museum and an excellent bookshop. In summer visitors throng the streets to see the castle, ancient church, the Grammar School and admire the delightful surrounding countryside.

*   *   *   *   *

Bury St Edmunds

Bury St Edmunds really is the Heart of East Anglia and one of the places at which Sigeberht, King of East Anglia, founded a monastry just prior to 640. Beodricksworth (St Edmund's Bury) is said by some writers to have been a Roman station, Villa Faustina; others have questioned this unsupported probability as no Roman remains have been found there. No archaeological evidence that there were any defences in Saxon times exists. The medieval town area can easily be traced because the names of the gates still remain in today's streets.

Baldwin of St Denis near Paris, who was personal physician to Edward the Confessor and later Abbot at Bury at the time of the Norman Conquest, was also a town planner. He designed a model town on a rectangular Roman grid plan to serve the Convent. By 1086 there were 342 houses on land formerly under the plough. Five gates were built into the walls, each with a chapel to Our Lady and a constant light burning. Outside the gates were wayfarers' hostels. The five gates of the town were pulled down about 1734 to improve access.

The town had a wall only on the western side which extended from West Gate to North Gate. The northern side, along the Tayfen (water) and the southern side, along the valley of the River Linnet, are protected by banks and ditches. The eastern side was defended by the walls of the Abbey and the River Lark. The East Gate adjoined the Abbot's Bridge guarding a ford and a foot bridge. Three different kinds of defence — two rivers, walling and the Abbey itself. In the Haberdeen, between the South Gate and the river, some earthworks may be seen, probably part of the defences. The line of the Grindle, an ancient earthwork, running due west from South Gate, was most likely part of the medieval or even earlier defences. In medieval times the Tayfen Water was a stream running from the river. Now that stream, long since gone, is replaced by Tayfen Road. Part at least of the Tayfen area must have been protected by walling as well as water. Excavations, by S. E. West M.A.,A.M.A., in 1968 at Tayfen Road revealed flint rubble wall with courses of thin red bricks. Mr. West said "There was some speculation as to the date of this wall. Accordingly a trench 30' × 10' was cut across the line of the wall to examine the foundation to establish the position of the Town Ditch. The excavation showed that the wall was an insertion into the earlier earthen rampart and that there was no evidence to suggest there had ever been any other wall on the site."

Tradition says that Canute built a ditch round the town. In fact a drawing of St Edmund's Abbey in the Moyse's Museum shows double dotted lines running round part of the perimeter of the Abbey from the junction with

This old engraving shows the site of Risbygate, where Risbygate Street meets St Andrews and Brentgovel Streets. Risbygate was removed in 1768.

Northgate Street and Mustow Street, round into Angel Hill, as far as St Margaret's Church. This is marked on the drawing as Canute's Ditch. Two bridge tracks lead across the ditch from St James' Church and the Norman Tower. This part of Canute's Ditch was purely a drainage ditch and nothing to do with defences.

Little remains of Bury's ancient defences — a chimney gap in the wall at East Gate, where it served a gate tower; a few stones at Tayfen; some earthworks at Haberdeen. North and South Gates have roundabouts; Risbygate Street where it meets Brentgovel Street and St Andrew's Street at the site of Risbygate has an untidy look. One interesting relic of former times lies in Risbygate Street, the Plague Stone which has a hollow into which vinegar was poured. The plague victims put money to cover their purchases into the vinegar to be collected by the retailer who delivered their goods near the stone. In this way contact between plague sufferers and others was avoided.

Present day Bury St Edmunds draws visitors from all over the world, mainly because of its abbey and the martyr king and since, in 1214, Cardinal Langton and the Barons swore at St Edmund's altar that they would obtain from King John the ratification of Magna Carta.

King Athelstan, grandson of Alfred the Great who had canonised Edmund, in 929 made a tour of the shrines of his kingdom. Alfred had minted coin with himself "Aelfred Rex." on one side and "Sc Eadmund Rex" on the other. On some he had even left his own name out. The Danes imitated these coins well before 890 and they were in use during Athelstan's visit to Bury in 929. This united Danes and Anglo-Saxons with both a common religion and a patron. One of Athelstan's clerks was Dunstan, the future saint and Archbishop of Canterbury who heard an eyewitness to the martyrdom, a seventy-five-year-old man who had been Edmund's armour bearer as a lad. One of Dunstan's auditors, Abbo of Fleury, recorded the events as told to him by Dunstan and dedicated the record to Dunstan in 985.

It is probable that the relics of Edmund were moved to Bury around 880. At this time Oswen, who had guarded the remains, and the ecclesiastical authorities, confirmed that the severed head had re-attached itself to the body and that the whole was incorrupt. Abbo, having seen the church which housed the relics, described it as enormous and wonderfully constructed of wood, in the use of which the East Anglians was particularly skilled. Verification that the body was incorrupt was made many times.

Protection of the relics led to their being taken to London and being brought back since the Archbishop of Canterbury seemed to be a greater threat to them than the Danes. From capture and fire the relics were thought to have been guarded but Houghton's researches and those of Edmond Bordier of France* trace them to the basilica of St Sernin, Toulouse. Stealing relics was a medieval pastime and losses were rarely admitted by those from whom the theft occurred. Cardinal Vaughan negotiated the return of the relics to England but unfortunately they never came back to their rightful resting place. They remain in the private chapel of the Duke of Norfolk at Arundel but the skull is still in Toulouse.

King Canute is famous through all time. He appears to have been a good man and did much to make amends for his father's ruthlessness. He reigned supreme from Gloucestershire to Murmansk in Russia, ruling Britain from 1016-35. He replaced the single guardian of the shrine with twenty Benedictine monks, under the Abbot Uvius.

The caring for the shrine was to continue for many years. In 1044, the second abbot in charge, Leofstan, overcome by curiosity opened the shrine to view the remains; because of this his hands shrivelled. Edward the Confessor, then king, sent Baldwin St Denis, his personal doctor, to tend the Abbot's hands and Baldwin stayed with him to guard the remains. In 1065 the town became known as St Edmundsbury, when a mint was established.

Sampson the tenth abbot was more fortunate than his predecessor, Leofstan. According to the monastery diarist of the time, Sampson opened the coffin in 1198 on the eve of the Feast of St Katherine, and 18 monks were witnessses to the event. The open coffin was "filled with the holy body . . . and the head lay united to the body on a small pillow."

On the 20th November, 1214, the anniversary of St Edmund's martyr-

* *Vivant Saint Edmond* by E. Bordier, Paris 1961.

dom, twenty-five English barons met at the Bury St Edmunds' Abbey, ostensibly on pilgrimage. On oath before the Archbishop of Canterbury, Stephen Langton at the High Altar, they swore to force the king to accept the Great Charter of Liberties. The following year at Runnymede King John signed the Magna Carta. The Magna Carta Trust, formed in 1957, under the auspices of Church, State, Parliamentarians, Ambassadors and the National Trust, sees that what the barons claimed for England in 1215 is preserved for all time. Magna Carta principles shall be perpetuated; Magna Carta sites be preserved; the Magna Carta shall be commemorated triennially.

Bury walls and gates saw bloodshed and fighting during the Black Death, exceptionally severe in Bury, in 1348-9. Because of the plague there was a shortage of priests and villeins available for monastic land work. This encouraged a system of leases and eventually led to the Peasants' Revolt. The revolt was suppressed. The Abbots were powerful later, after the Peasants' Revolt, their power with that of the Government of the day was paramount and Bury was the only English town not to receive a national amnesty.

A fire raged in the Monastery on 20th January 1465 when the spire sank down into the tower. The fire spread along the roof of the choir and the canopy caught alight and fell on to the shrine. The cross-beam over the shrine and the shirt and Oswen's casket, containing nail and hair parings, and the shrine itself, when the fire was extinguished, were all found to be intact.

James I gave Bury St Edmunds armorial bearings: on the scroll is the motto *Sacrarium Regis, Cunabua Legis* meaning the Shrine of a King, Cradle of the Law. Thus for all time are St Edmund and Magna Carta linked. The shield bears, on a blue ground, three gold crowns each of which is pierced by two silver downward pointing arrows. The crest on the gold and blue wreath is a sitting or sejant wolf, holding between its forepaws the crowned decapitated head of Edmund.

William Cobbett called it "The Nicest Town in the World", and it is a nice town to this day, a town steeped in history.

A chimney gap in the wall at East Gate, Mustow Street, Bury St Edmunds, where it served a gate tower.

5. East Coast Defences

CAISTER-BY-YARMOUTH — GREAT YARMOUTH — SOUTHWOLD — DUNWICH — HARWICH — TILBURY

Caister-by-Yarmouth

IN THE summer of 1951 Charles Green began what was thought to be two months excavation at an area west of Brooke Avenue, at Caister-by-Yarmouth.* In fact the dig proved to be of such importance that the excavation continued until 1955. Much of the site was excavated but only 1/35th of the total area has been left to public view and the rest of the one-time seaport lies beneath modern housing and roads.

Caister-by-Yarmouth was a small Roman town built beside a sheltered harbour in about 125 A.D. Charles Green said there is little doubt that the whole port of Caistor was known as Gariannonum, from the mouth of the Gariens or Yare. Now the name is used for Burgh Castle fort only, while the name Caister is used for the walled town.

During the third and fourth century the port had brisk trade with the Rhineland, after which time shrinkage of trade led to the port's decay. The town became deserted by the early fifth century and two hundred years later an Anglo-Saxon settlement replaced the old Roman town. As late as the seventh century Caister harbour was still in use and ship remains of that period have been found. By the time of the Danish settlement in A.D. 880, dry marsh pastures had appeared due to the silt banks rising above high tide level. Therefore because the harbour was not usable the Danes and the Normans remained nearer the sea by the mouth of the Bure.

Caister harbour was well placed being protected all round except from the south east. It was seldom lashed by gales, being protected from the north east, the prevailing, winds.

Five miles south west across Breydon Water is Burgh Castle, the true Gariannonum. Burgh Castle is one of the Saxon Shore Forts of East Anglia.

---

*Also known as Caister, Caister-near-Yarmouth and, more recently, Caister-on-Sea.

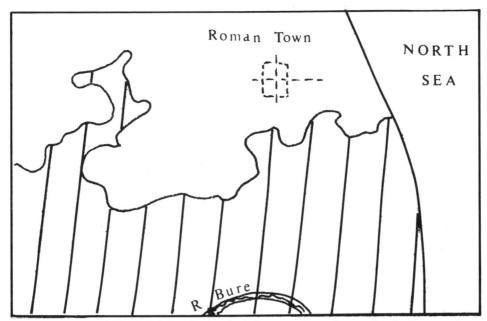

A marine transgression map shows, by its shaded area, where the sea lay in Roman times
This later became marsh pasture and is now built over with roads and houses.

Now it stands well back from the sea but originally it was on a tidal peninsula on, what is now, Breydon Water. Brancaster (Branodunum) on the north Norfolk coast and Bradwell, probably the Roman Othona, in Essex, standing beside a nuclear power station on the Blackwater estuary, were two others.

At the end of the third century A.D. the Romans built a series of mighty forts along the south-east coast of Britain. Then ten forts existed, possibly eleven, but only nine survive today. These are the famous Litus Saxonicum — the Forts of the Saxon Shore. They were erected near or at the edge of the sea; at river or harbour mouths, where maximum defence was possible and the harbours provided access for the Roman fleet. Communication between the forts was made up and down the coast by sea as few of the forts were sited near large Roman roads.

Various reasons have been suggested for these forts. It was thought they were built against the Saxon sea-raiders, harrying the Low Countries, northern France and the British coasts. A later theory, very well researched, suggests that the forts were built against a proposed invasion by Roman forces, on the shores of Britain. At the time when the forts were built Carausius, a Belgic mariner, rebelled against Maximian, co-regent of Diocletian. Rebelling as he did against Rome he took his fleet with him and made himself Emperor, taking control of Britain for seven years. Accordingly he set up his Forts of the Saxon Shore against the day when Maximian would return to reconquer Britain — hence the expected invasion. Indeed this would explain the massive size of the forts, which were far too large to be necessary to control forces already on the coast, or against Saxon invaders, whose strength in the third century was not very great. In A.D. 193 Carausius was murdered and three years later Roman forces landed on the Hampshire coast thus by-passing the Saxon Shore Forts. So Rome ruled once more. After this period the forts were probably used against the Saxon raiders. At that time Roman signal stations were built around the coast to supplement the Saxon Shore Forts.

Of the nine surviving forts, Richborough, Pevensey and Porchester are rich in remains while others are comparatively poor ruins like Burgh Castle. At the castle Sigeberht, King of the East Angles, is said to have come in 630 A.D., to give the land inside the Roman fortress to St Fursa, an Irish ascetic, and here supposedly a monastery was founded, called Cnobheresburg. Built during the Dark Ages, its history, as indeed that of the castle itself, is shrouded in the darkness of uncertainty — little is known.

The Roman Imperial authorities in the times of Hadrian founded the new town which was later named Caister. The earliest Roman defences were timber palisades and clay ramparts, soon built over with a ten foot thick wall of flint. The area enclosed by the walls was some thirty acres in extent, the seaport standing on high ground above the estuary and harbour. Outside the walls a paved road ran from the South Gate to the harbour. This road led over a bridge across the triple ditches and banks which surrounded the town, leading in turn to the quay and harbour, then only some four hundred yards away.

Caister-by-Yarmouth, it has been suggested, was the only Roman commercial seaport in Britain. It was certainly important in the second century A.D., being the shortest and therefore the cheapest sea crossing to the Rhine mouth, for it was at that time Britain imported glass and pottery from the Rhineland.

Beside the Caister-Norwich road (A1064), Caister Roman Camp is now open to the public. The remains of this second century Roman seaport, a few hundred yards from the traffic lights, is almost hidden by a lay-by and a wire fence. Few people would realize that here lies an important piece of Norfolk history.

Compared with many Roman camps there is not a lot to see and the site may well disappoint visitors. A kitchen, a dining room, granary and vestibule

Reconstruction of Caister by Yarmouth Roman Camp by Alan Sorrell, 1972. *Norwich Museums*

have been marked by walls in some places only a few inches high. There are the ruins of a guard chamber to the South Gate, which led down to the quay and harbour some four hundred yards distant. A section of Town Wall ten feet wide is partly marked with flint, partly with gravel. Several concrete circles show where piles probably supported a bridge across the moat. A section of a main road is also marked out on the ground. Remains of a large building inside the South Gate is thought to have been a hostel for seamen. Part of one bank and ditch is visible.

Alan Sorrell made an excellent reconstruction of Caister-by-Yarmouth Roman Camp in 1972. Used in conjunction with my small marine transgression map, it shows clearly where the sea once lay, and how ships came right into the protected harbour in Roman times. The shaded part of the map shows the sea which later became marsh pasture. Today much of the land is a built up area with roads and housing.

Despite the lack of impact, this site is well worth a visit. Knowledge of history and imagination can stimulate mental pictures of Roman sailors and tradesmen walking on the main street which is laid out in plan on the ground. Bank and ditch, the inner ones of the triple protection, can be imagined deeper as they once were. Roman ships sail into harbour, drop anchor and disgorge their cargoes and men.

*   *   *   *   *   *

Great Yarmouth

Reasonable historical records of Yarmouth exist and these mark the value of coastal defences to an island race.

On 28th September, 1260 Henry III granted a licence to the burgesses of Yarmouth "to enclose the town with a wall and foss (moat) as long as the said burgesses towards us and our heirs shall well and faithfully behave themselves." But nothing happened for twenty-four years and in all the walls took one hundred and thirty-six years to complete. In fact the plague of 1349 severely affected the inhabitants of Yarmouth and the countryside. The walls were not built for defensive purposes only, but also to prevent traders from bringing their wares by stealth and escaping the customary tolls. The new gates made it easy for the gate-keepers to see each vessel coming into the city. Henry Manship* said, "The walls of a town or city be necessary in three respects: first, for comliness; secondly for safety of the inhabitants; thirdly, for terror of the enemy." Yarmouth walls were built and finished with a fair high wall, em-

---

**History of Yarmouth*, Henry Manship, 1619.

battled, and most magnificently towered, and turreted exceedingly comely; and in like manner to this day continued accordingly."

An old map from Palmer's book* clearly shows that in ancient times the sea flowed in as far as Norwich. It gives an idea too, how necessary it was during the time Yarmouth walls were in use, to defend the large expanse of river to the west. The sands where Yarmouth stands had earlier silted up and stopped the sea encroaching inland. Even when in medieval times the water had dwindled to river size, there was a need to defend the town from the open river and marsh area.

The town wall had a perimeter of about 2,238 yards, with ten gates and sixteen towers; opinions vary about this, but these figures are the most accepted. The building was begun on the east side, probably at the North East Tower, in St Nicholas' churchyard, and proceeded southwards. It is presumed that the work finished at the north end of the town. There is a tradition that the north gate was built by the person or persons who had amassed considerable sums of money by burying the dead during the time of the plague. When the walls were completed a moat or ditch was dug all round, with bridges to each gate. This moat was so complete that boats could pass with their cargoes to all parts of the town, for the convenience of trade and commerce. The magistrates were careful to keep the moat clean from rubbish, stones, and earth, and people so offending were heavily fined. "Thus the town being fortified with a wall and moat, towers, gates and bars, was deemed a sufficient defence against all assailants with bows and arrows, flings, battering-rams, and all other missive engines of those times."

"Of all towns within these parts, walled alone is she;
Lest she to foes continually, a scrambling prey might be.
Whereby, herself and all the coast, she doth full well defend.
God grant that still she may so do, even to the world's end."

For supporting and carrying on this expensive work, the inhabitants were empowered to collect a custom called murage, on all imports and exports. The murage was at a set rate, and in force for a certain time, which was renewable at the end of each term, at the king's pleasure.

The service of work and labour done by the inhabitants and adjoining tenants in building or repairing the walls of a city or castle was called *murorum operatio*, that is, wall-work. When this personal duty was commuted into money, the tax gathered to cover the expenses was called murage. Many old bills for work on the walls at that time still exist, expenses of the murage.

"Bought of John Neve, two small boats of stone, price 2s. And for porterage of the same stones, 4d. Also bought of William Lister de Acle, one

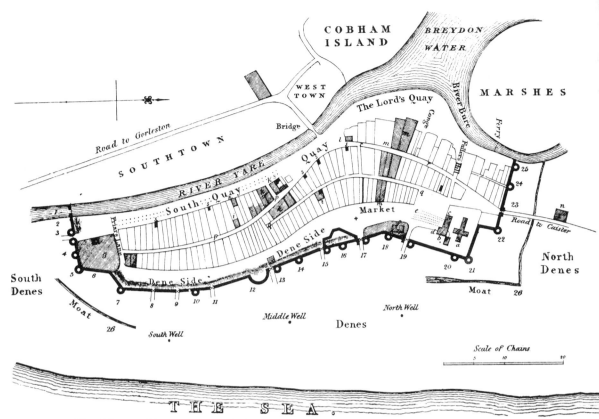

The old map of Great Yarmouth showing walled defences with gates and towers. 1-River boom, 2-South Mount, 3-South Gate, 4-First Tower, 5-Friar Tower, 6-Ravelin, 7-South East Tower, 8-Second Gate, 9-Third Gate, 10-Fourth Gate, 11-Little Mount, 12-A walled up Gate, 13-Fifth Gate, 14-Sixth Tower, 15-Sixth Gate, 16-Guard Tower, 17-Market Gate, 18-Hospital Tower, 19-Pudding Gate, 20-Twelfth Tower, 21-King Henry's Tower, 22-Fourteenth Tower, 23-North Gate, 24-Fifteen Tower, 25-North West Tower, 26-The Moat.

boat of white rock stones, price 7s. 6d. And for porterage of the same, 1s. 3d. Bought of Valiniana de Wutton, of Norwich, 200 treys of lime, the price of each trey 3d. halfpenny, and in measurement thereof 12 treys, whereof the sum of the money is £3.10d. And for porterage of the same lime at times £1.1s. And for making the same into mortar, 3d. Bought of Richard Perles 5 lasts of bricks, the price of each last £1.3s. and besides for advantage 2500. Whereof the sum of the money is £5.15s And for porterage of the same at times, 13s. 1d. halfpenny. Also paid to William de Weston, and William de Seiter, the same year, masons, for the building of eleven rods upon the wall, the height of 16 feet of men from the foundation upwards, and for the cover of a certain gate, whereof the sum appears to be £8.5s.7d. Also paid by the hands of the wardens aforesaid, for 300 of iron, and 5 garbs (a garb of steel consisted of 30 pieces), of steel, bought for spades and tools for the braking down of the said old wall, granted for the said murage, the price of each hundred of iron 5s. and of each garb of steel, 8d."*

Yarmouth was built in the form of an oblong quadrangle of 133 acres, on a peninsula; it is encompassed on the south and east by the sea, and on the north by the land, and on the west by the Yare over which there was a handsome drawbridge, built in 1427 before which there had been only a ferryboat. The drawbridge was built at the expense of £2,150. This bridge divided the town from Suffolk. Yarmouth had four main streets running north and south, intersected by 156 narrow lanes or rows. This former Cinque Port was surrounded by a wall on the east, north and south sides, with 10 gates and 16 towers.

The old Ministry of Works, when they excavated, revealed the unique method of wall building in this ancient town. Yarmouth lies on a sandbank which originally stood in the middle of an estuary, now Breydon Water. The walls were 23 feet high, with the towers and turrets even higher still, and today Yarmouth walls still give this feeling of tremendous height. In 1544, during the wars against France and Scotland, the King, through the Duke of Norfolk, commanded that, "first disgardening such gardens as were all alongst with the walls of Yarmouth builded he caused them to be rampired," using sand from the Denes outside. So within a space of fifteen weeks, for *multus manibus levatur opus*, "many hands make light work", Yarmouth was strongly fortified against the enemy.

For one hundred and fifty years the walls served their purpose but in 1547 Henry VIII, still at war, sent the Duke of Norfolk to inspect the fortifications and was not pleased. Sandhills, continually shifting, had grown so high as to dominate the town and squatters had built huts against the walls. The Duke ordered the huts to be pulled down, the dunes levelled, the moat cleaned out and the inside walls backed with earth, which explains the sharp drop in level from Deneside today.

"In May of the same year three tall barks or man of war, were riding in the Yarmouth roads, pretending to have a letter of marque from Chatillion, the French admiral. Whereupon the town discharged the great ordnance against them, and with a sacre from off the walls, did strike the said admiral's ship half a yard above water, whereby she was enforced to steer off, without gun-shot." [†]A few days later the ship perished.

In 1549 a body of Kett's followers were refused admittance to Yarmouth by the townspeople, who also refused to supply them with beer. Kett brought six cannons from Lowestoft to the north end of Gorleston, intending to fire on

*Extract of 1336

[†] C. J. Palmer, 1872.

South East Tower on Blackfriars Road, the best known Yarmouth tower.

the town from there but the move was not unobserved. Townsmen were detached to set fire to a large stack of hay, on the west side of the Haven, from which the northerly wind drove the smoke towards the guns allowing the men of Yarmouth to advance unseen. Thirty prisoners and the cannons were captured. The rebels retaliated by destroying Haven materials stored by the walls and then marched across the Denes to the South Gate. Beaten back by cannon fire from the walls and mounts, they fled and never again returned.

In April 1569 Queen Elizabeth I sent to Yarmouth "demy culverins, of cast iron, mounted and furnished, 3; sacres of cast iron, likewise mounted and furnished, 2; minions of cast iron, in like sort mounted, 3; curriers compleat, with flasks and touch boxes, 50; pikes 50; bows 50; arrows 50; sheafs 50; demy-culvering shot 200; sacre-shot 300; minion shot 300; serpentine powder 600 weight; corn powder one C weight; match one C weight." During this time when cannon fire was available, the arrow slits in the walls were blocked up and gunports were built to take the cannons.

During the time of the Spanish Armada (1588), Queen Elizabeth ordered Norwich to pay £333 and Norfolk and Suffolk £971 towards the cost of repairing Yarmouth walls. She sent £300 worth of gunpowder and demy culverins and granted a licence to build an artillery yard where weapons could be stored, where Theatre Plain now stands. A boom was constructed across the river near the South Gate. Two jetties were built which held a chain across the Haven at a cost of £107 - 15s. Two men, Thomas Fletcher and Walter Barret, were appointed to take charge and to see that the boom was shut and opened at convenient times but it had to remain closed between dusk and dawn. Between the boom and the river a large mound was built, higher than the walls on which several cannon were placed.

86

A lookout of four men scanned the horizon from the church tower every day while the townspeople manned the walls. On St George's Road, the original road leading to the jetty, is part of the mount, the most important point in the defence of the town. Here with its battered revetment and sloping parapet is the only remains of a town wall ravelin still existing in England.

At one time there was a walk around the inside of the walls. In 1601 the Corporation ordered that the inhabitants of Yarmouth should have the walk reinstated with all the stopped places opened, but sand encroachment continued and it became impossible to restore the walls or the walk. By 1621 the walls were no longer kept up, and the towers passed into private hands. Each time a threat passed the walls were neglected. In 1625 Charles I fearing invasion sent a commission to inspect the defences. It was reported that to replace the boom at the South Gate would cost £120, and to extend the wall to take two guns commanding the harbour entrance £10. It was also advised that "a murdering piece" be planted on the east tower of South Gate and most other towers.

At the outbreak of the Civil War, Yarmouth proclaimed for Parliament. Thinking that the Royalists would attack from the north the walls were strengthened and the deepest moat was widened from the North West Tower to Pudding Gate. This was the last time the walls were put in a state of defence as the development of artillery rendered the walls obsolete. They remained as a defensive structure, however, until the late eighteenth century.

The North West Tower at Great Yarmouth.

The sixteenth century North West Tower, with a conical pantile roof, stands beside the Yare a few yards from the water's edge. Being unsafe it is now closed to the public, and the walling on either side has been demolished. The wall originally ran along Rampart Road and there was a second tower, but neither exist today. North Gate was sixty feet wide and was removed in 1807. From the site of the North Gate the first remaining stretch of wall still stands to its full height, from North Road. At the end of this wall section the North East Tower stands at the corner of Town Way Road. Here the wall turns at right angles and backs onto houses on the main Norwich/Caister road and outside the wall is a children's playground, with St Nicholas' church behind. At the end of the wall is King Henry's Tower which was once a charnel house.

St Nicholas' Gate was made through a tower of the same name, and was removed in 1799 to enlarge the churchyard. Beyond that was Pudding Gate which was but a small foot-passage through a twenty-four foot wide tower. A plaque on the wall of the Hospital School commemorates the gate. The Hospital Tower is somewhat hidden behind the gates and surrounding buildings in a narrow lane. Here outside the walls a slaughter house was built in early times and one still exists today. Beyond the wall, on the inside of the defence, at this point is a non-Conformist cemetery, surrounded by Town Wall, Hospital School wall, factories and the backs of shops. An opening in the Town Wall, an enlarged arrowslit, emits the sounds of beasts waiting below in the slaughter-house.

Market Gate was made under Market Tower and both together were fifty-four feet wide. The gateway was pointed in a square tower, with a trackway running through to the sea, called Market Road Way. Now the new Market Gates Shopping Centre is built up and over the old wall dwarfing it into red brick obscurity.

Guard Tower, outside the wall, is today overshadowed by large modern buildings. Oxney's, Steele's or Theatre Gate once had a conical roof with a weather vane dated 1680. The gate stood at Regent Street and a road once ran past it to the Denes, past Middle Well and a nearby windmill. Pinnacles Tower also had a sixteenth century conical roof. Share's Tower was twenty-seven feet wide and beside it stood Chapel Gate where today Trafalgar Road joins the hospital. The Gate was demolished in 1776 and the area widened by removing part of the wall.

Main Tower was different, since it was a wall, higher than the Town Wall, surrounding an internal mount which was a rampart known as New or East Mount. Remains of this, the most important of the one-time ramparts of the Yarmouth defences, are still to be seen at the back of the hospital. The outside can be viewed from a narrow alley behind houses on St George's Road and the inside section from behind a locked door inside the hospital itself. In Tudor times part of the old wall here was demolished and rebuilt as the Main Tower to house this roughly triangular shaped mound which jutted out in an easterly direction from the wall.

Little Mount Gate stood opposite present day York Road. Harris or Baldry's Tower today has a bedroom built on top of it as part of a house fronting onto Deneside. The lower part of the tower serves as a cellar to the house. A small iron door outside at the bottom of the tower was where rope was pulled through from a nearby rope works. Nearby stood Ropemaker's Gate and between this gate and Harris Tower ropemakers plied their trade, spinning twine on the Twine Ground outside the walls.

Garden Gate stood across Alma Road by the small Jewish cemetery and was a mere six feet wide. Something of what may have been its former charm still lingers at the gate site today. From the site of the Garden Gate onwards to the south, the wall rises again, in places, to its full height. Just beyond is the South East Tower, one of the best known, most picturesque and certainly the most illustrated of the towers. Twenty-one feet wide, it is a typical Yarmouth tower, with the wall forming the flat side of the semi-circular bastion. The top section of the South East Tower is decorated with a chequer board of brick and flint, the decorating being carried out when the original arrowslits were replaced by cannon ports.

Two huge stretches of walling reach to the Black Friars Tower, where in 1588 a rampart was built to the east of the tower. A passageway, still there, was cut through the tower in 1807. Palmer's Tower, some few hundred yards along the wall which runs at right angles to Black Friars, stands behind the end of well renovated terraced houses whose back gardens face the wall.

South Gate has a single portal and two flanking towers. The road through the gate led only to the Denes, that track of sand lying between the sea and the river, but the site was no doubt of importance from a defensive point of view. Beyond the gate a final stretch of wall ended at the river. The last remains of this part of the ancient wall lie, recently buried, under a cascade of builders' rubble, scrap iron and old refrigerators.

Today Yarmouth walls have been opened up wherever possible as old buildings have been demolished from their surfaces. For the most part they are in excellent repair, a credit to the foresight of the city fathers. Lawns, gardens and paths have been laid out wherever possible. Handsome, massive decorative and intensely interesting, these walls should not be missed by anyone interested in defences.

*   *   *   *   *   *

Southwold

Southwold is a charming old world town which always seems to be bathed in sun. South it certainly is not, being on the east coast of Suffolk. Nor is the word wold applicable in the twentieth century, for wold means an elevated tract of open uncultivated country or moorland. For all that it still has nine green open spaces, some with flowers and trees, others just grassy places: Skilman's Hill and Gun Hill; North, South and East Green; St Edmund's and St James' Green; and swards named Barnaby and Bartholomew. So perhaps after all wold is not so inappropriate. One charming name is lost now, that of Tibby's Green, now St Edmund's, after tibbys or calves kept on the green because they were too young to be allowed to roam on Southwold Common. These greens were a result of a great fire in 1659 when 238 buildings were destroyed and never rebuilt.

Called Sudwold, Southwold, Swole or Southole, the town was not as great in antiquity as Dunwich, but greater in navigation and traffic as a port.

Southwold received a grant of murage coupled with a licence to crenellate in 1250, but no traces of this or of the sixteenth century fortifications, which were to isolate the town by a wall on the landward side, remain. Very little is known about Southwold defences.

The town has a long, but so far as we know, not an ancient history. A Charter was granted by Henry VII, containing one edict which was that a three day fair should be held on South Green on Trinity Monday and the two following days.

Gun Hill is the most famous of the Greens, named for the six guns, supplied by George II, which have stood there, except for a period during the Second World War, ever since. They are the guns asked for by the town, in the latter part of 1745, to defend the town. The guns are embellished with the Tudor rose and crown. The late Major General P. J. Mackesy, in his booklet, *The Southwold Guns*, points out that the rose and crown was in use for such weapons from about 1485 until 1711, some 226 years. Mackesy suggests they were cast in Elizabeth I's reign and that they were old when they first came to Southwold. The Duke of Cumberland's involvement in their provision is restricted to his uncertain arrival in Aldeburgh on 17th October 1745, reported by Gardner, on his way home from the Low Countries. Perhaps at this time the Duke was asked to use his influence with the king in support of their petition. Certainly Cumberland after Culloden, fought on 16th April 1746, returned to London overland. In any case they could not have been Prince Charles Edward's because he was not equipped with such guns and the only eighteen pounders he had were French ones. The photostat of a Minute of Board of Ordnance 24th December, 1745, detailing ordnance and stores to be

The Battle of Sole Bay. The English Fleet engaging the Dutch.
Reproduced by Gracious Permission of Her Majesty the Queen

sent to Southwold, and other photostats of other relevant Orders etc. are at the Southwold Town Hall.

Gardner says, "Southwold was a town on a hill. The east was bounded by the German Ocean, other ways almost surrounded by the river Blyth, on the north west is a bridge formerly a Draw-bridge for a passage into the town." If there was a drawbridge there must have been a wall, bank or defence of some kind. "On the cliffs there are two batteries, one a regular fortification having a good parapet with six guns. Near the parapet was an ancient fort. On the North a pair of Butts for exercising of bow and arrow. Fire beacons stood on the South part of the hill called Eye Cliff." Thomas Gardner, a Salt Officer and chronicler of both Southwold and Dunwich, died in 1769 and lies buried in St Edmunds' Church, Southwold.

The guns which saw use throughout history in a number of ways also saw tragedy. Firing a birthday salute for the Prince of Wales, later Edward VII, in 1842, was undertaken by the Preventive Officer with a volunteer detachment of his men. When reloading Number One gun for the second round the charge exploded in the bore and instantly killed James Martin, a married man with three children.

Southwold was shelled in the First World War by the Germans who, seeing the guns, thought it was of fortified importance. The guns were hidden away during the last war to prevent a repetition of this blunder and to save them being used for scrap. Bombs certainly fell on undefended Southwold during the Second World War and most of the townspeople were evacuated. The place became a prohibited area and shops and houses were boarded up. However in 1959 the guns were re-mounted on wooden copies of the old mountings and they stand now as they did for the previous two hundred years.

A battle took place in 1672 between an Anglo-French fleet under James, Duke of York and a Dutch fleet under Admiral de Ruyter. This was the Battle of Solebay, an older name for Southwold Bay. On 27th May the Dutch, in the early hours of the morning, found the opposing fleet on a lee shore. The Earl of Sandwich, commanding the northern Blue Squadron, died when his flagship, the *Royal James*, was lost. The Dutch claimed the victory since they had prevented the English fleet crossing the North Sea to co-operate with the French in the Netherlands and the English because they held the seas when the Dutch withdrew. Perhaps it is more accurate to say things were even. The French fleet pulled away from the lee shore to the south and took little part in the action.

The town took in the wounded of both sides which entailed a large bill for nursing the sick and dying and the expenses fell to the town because the king never paid the bill.

The Town Sign commemorates the Battle of Solebay which I think is beautiful. The sign shows the Duke of York's ship, the *Royal Prince*, attacking the *Seven Provencien* and the motto "defend they ryght". Southwold town lies in its quietness behind Gun Hill, smooth lawns, tastefully converted houses, seeming never to have stirred from its pleasant silence.

*   *   *   *   *   *

Dunwich

On the north side Dunwich was protected by the River Blyth whose mouth was then south of where it is today; this made access in some places dangerous and in others less difficult. To prevent infiltration that way several artificial mounds were cast up on the ridge and these were fenced with palisades adjacent to the Palesdike. To the east an earthen rampart was made, fortified on top with timber palisades, with, at its foot outside the city, a deep ditch, as an additional defence. Later much of this rampart was taken down and the ditch filled in and levelled with the ground, to take the wall of Grey Friars Monastery. The town ramparts with their ditch was the western boundary of the town, and earthworks may still be found on Westleton Common.

Agnes Strickland wrote of Dunwich in the seventeenth century—
"Fair Dunwich! thou art lowly now,
Renowned and sought no more."

Indeed the latter is true three hundred years later.

The riches and prosperity of the old City of Dunwich were largely due to the sea: ship-building and fishing provided trade with towns in East Anglia and abroad. In medieval times Dunwich exported cloth to Iceland, Hull and France, pitch, tar, steel and fur to Norway, Finland and Sweden and wool to Germany. It imported cloth from Hamburg, steel from France, salt from Brittany and steel and skins from Spain. Today, gone are the harbour, the ships, the trading flags and the hustle-bustle of commerce.

Dunwich was conquered by the Saxons; plundered by the Danes; recorded in Domesday Survey; saw troubles caused by Henry VIII at the Dissolution; witnessed the Battle of Solebay; there were even tigers in Dunwich woods seven hundred years ago. Once the town, like many other places on the East Anglian coast, had its smugglers and the defensive walls guarded against the law breaker as well as the enemy.

The discovery of a coarse earthenware pot containing silver and brass coins of the Roman era seem to be a confirmation of Roman occupation. Evidence seems to suggest that Roman spur roads led to Dunwich. One being from Caistor St Edmunds, Venta Icenorum, another was traced from a heath at Dunwich across country to Bury St Edmunds. This latter may have been an

This track with the bridge over it was once Middle Street, Dunwich. The dip in the far distance is at the cliff edge.

ancient British trackway. Dunwich may in Roman times have been part of the east coast defence system, as it lay half way between Burgh and Walton. If a Roman town or fort was built there it most certainly is now under the sea.

Throughout its history Dunwich must have witnessed many battles. In 1173 Prince Henry, rebelling against his father, Henry II, joined by Robert Earl of Leicester and 300 Flemings was reputed to have attempted a landing at Dunwich but was repelled. They landed down the coast and tried to take the city from the landward side but again failed. A manuscript poem of Jordan Fantosme, a monk of the time, says,

"Within the town was neither maid nor wife
Who did not carry a stone to the palisade for throwing
Thus did the people of Dunwich defend themselves
As these verses tell which are here written
And so brave were great and small
That Earl Robert retired completely mocked."

The drift of shingle from north to south led to the obstruction and movement of the outlets of all rivers in the area and Dunwich was no exception. During King Henry III's reign (1216-1272), the harbour silted up and the king gave the town £57. 10s for preventative measures. During the reign of Edward I (1272-1307), the town returned to importance with ships fishing off Iceland. In 1328 a spit of shingle and sand covered Dunwich Haven making it useless. For over a hundred years Dunwich tried to revive the lost trade, but at last the old port ceased to function in 1640.

Dunwichers were often at fault in raiding the Orkney Islands enroute to "Ysland" as it was known in old records. The ships were well armed with weapons as well as fishing gear, sometimes carrying sarpetres, hackebushes, bows, arrows, gunpowder, along with beer, flitches of bacon, wheat and salt. One wonders what the Cod War was like in those byegone days.

Dunwich was a splendid city, according to Thomas Gardiner's *Historical Account of Dunwich*, 1754, "in all a mile square, surrounded with a stone wall and having brazen gates." He says, Dunwich had "52 churches, chapels, religious houses, a hospital, a King's palace, a Bishop's seat, a mayor's mansion, several windmills and a mint." Dunwich walls were a very strong fortification at that time with approaches through gate houses, "Howsed over, and strongly gated", so that, "the towne was a grete forse, strong enoughe to keep out a great number of people."

The Domesday Book records a manor of two carrucates, of which one was carried away by the sea between the time of King Edward the Confessor and Edward I. A carrucate was as much as a team of oxen could plough in a season — about 100 acres, so this loss was a large one. In 1347 some 400 houses and part of the city wall and other buildings fell into the sea during a great storm. In 1385 a great storm swept away the churches of St Leonard, St Martin and St Nicholas. In 1570 damage, described as "incredible" was again caused by the sea.

All that now remains of Dunwich are a few houses; part of the ruins of Grey Friars Monastery; a small section of the town ditch; and a solitary tombstone, dedicated to the memory of John Brinkley Easey, aged 23, 1823, a few yards from the cliff edge. Gardner tells us that by 1540 not a quarter of the town was left standing. The erosion continues.

The Dunwich Seal was granted to the city by King John in the first charter of 1199. This is the earliest example of a medieval ship and has a special place in naval architecture. It shows the fore and aft fighting stages as small structures on posts inside the high ends of the hull. These were but temporary structures placed in merchant ships during time of war.

Present day visitors to Dunwich will find the remains of the defences of the town, now but a sleepy village, inland of the old city, by walking and climbing at the top of the cliffs. A narrow track through the woods beside Grey Friars ruins is the one-time Middle Street of Dunwich City, and there is part of an ancient town ditch nearby. Anti-tank blocks line part of the shore and straddle the estuary, remnants of the Second World War, standing sentinel on the beach where once they defended the village, river and hinterland. A lone pill-box stands beside the beach cafe. The track which was Middle Street may be found opposite the signpost to Westleton. A recent bridge crosses this old "street" which leads only to broken cliffs, the sea and inevitable watery destruction. From the beach below it is easy to see where Middle Street stood because of the gap in the cliff at that point.

The North East Essex Sub Aqua Club launched a project in 1971 to search and record Dunwich under the sea. Stuart Bacon of the club, in conjunction with J. I. Carter, wrote a book, *Ancient Dunwich*, from his diving log. The world of the under-water diver is beset with problems and difficulties, not least of all the cold and gloom. The ruins of old churches and buildings have been re-discovered and carefully recorded, despite visibility of as little as six to twelve inches, or just complete blackness. One of the city gates was found, assumed to be the Western Middle Gate, once situated along Duck Street. The ruins are in twenty to twenty-five feet of water on moving sand and heaped on the seabed.

Most people coming to East Anglia hear tales about Dunwich church bells ringing under the sea. John Day, who sailed barges along the Dunwich coast, is said to have known his position by the sound of the submerged Dunwich bell. Whole churches have disappeared into the sea at Dunwich

Dunwich map by Thomas Gardner, 1753 Shows; A-Rampart; F-Duck Street; G-Middlegate; H-Mid Gate Street; I-All Saints Church; L-Grey Friars; c-Old Quay; d-Old Port; 13-Cliff line, 1753; Heavy Line (B), here added, was the cliff line in 1976.

overnight and a strong belfrey, with bell still hung, might stand for a time under the sea and the tide's movement could well ring the bell. In such a situation the sound of the bell could be carried ashore by light summer breezes.

*   *   *   *   *   *

Harwich

The Romans were in Harwich at the conquest in AD 43, and Roman pottery and tiles have been unearthed. Morant in his *History and Antiquities of the County of Essex* mentions the Roman camp which once stood on Beacon

96

Hill. A tumulus also seen on the hill points to an earlier time in history. The same site was later used in defence against the Saxons.

Harwich did not rise to prominence until the twelfth century when floods changed the direction of the river making Dovercourt, previously important, redundant. The efforts of Roger Bigod, the fourth Earl of Norfolk, compelling Ipswich bound shipping to use Harwich, by confiscating steering apparatus, sails and other equipment and pulling their ships on to dry land, did a great deal to make Harwich a powerful seaport.

In 1338 Edward III granted to Harwich, which intended to enclose the town with a wall, a murage for five years on goods for sale, coming by land or water, to their town. There had long been rivalry between Harwich and Ipswich because the former interfered with the latter's shipping, and of this Ipswich had repeatedly complained. Now they complained again, and the grant was stopped. Harwich continued to exact tolls on shipping and the King, seeing the need to defend the town, gave his support. During the reign of Richard II a murage was granted to build walls and a castle at the north-east corner of the town. The castle must have been built because permission to exact toll for the repair of the castle was granted during the reign of Henry IV, (1399-1413).

Old maps of the town walls exist, and a small section of the septaria wall is still extant in St Nicholas' churchyard. An alleyway to the back of a pub on the other side of the churchyard wall also shows this large chunk of masonry. From its position on the map of the Harwich Town Wall this strip of wall must have been the actual width of the wall, which means that it was about fifteen feet thick. Few records mention the walls, so little appears to be known of their building or use. In 1539 the Earl of Oxford visited Harwich to find the people had made trenches and bulwarks, and he commented on the women and children at work on the bulwarks. Women were often to be found doing manual tasks such as wheeling and carrying gravel and soil to build quays, digging ditches and cleaning the dunghills outside the gate.

A stone cliff was some kind of defence from the sea at Harwich, as well as the sea wall defending the marsh pasture. But in 1551 three great tides broke down this sea wall and marsh and town were flooded. All Harwich citizens who had, or were ever likely to have cattle pastured there, were asked to pay towards repairing the marsh wall.

The weather and rough seas were often a defender of Harwich in medieval times, warding off a number of attacks which otherwise might have caused loss of life. But court records show that on two occasions damage and death did take place. In 1450 "the town was spoiled and destroyed by our ene- mies, and our neighbours to the number of nine were slaughtered," and in the same year "Adam Palmer showed to our French enemies the very secret way of our port of Orwell, leading their ships in safety to the grave damage of the town."

In 1553, one William Russel received 20d. for using his lighter to bring in salsers, bumbards, demi-culverins and shovels to widen the ditches. And Katherine Harrison received 21d. " for half a bushel of beer that the labourers did drink that wrought in the ditches at the town gates." Payments were made for "lead to cover the touch-holes; for iron bolts; for canvas to make nail shot and sayl needles to sow the pokes of nail shot."

In the same year work was done on Goodman Tilney's Gate, St Helen's Gate, Baryon's Gate and Savers (?)*Gate and on the marsh wall, and a key and lock bought for the stocks for 4d. A lock was also bought for the turnpike for the constables, "for that they dyd occupy it about ye turne peke (turnpike) at ye towne gattes when ye bessynes was at ye Resynge of Dudle agenste ye quen," 4d. In 1557 a Council order sent one of the lords to inspect the defective fort at Harwich and negotiate with the townspeople to subscribe to the fort's repair, asking that if the queen had it repaired, would they keep it in proper condition. But the bargain was not kept. Dunkirkers, French priva-teers, could enter Harwich harbour easily, burn the 50 to 60 ships which were usually in port at one time, and landing but a few men burn down the town. Knowing this possibility 3,000 men were sent in and in August, the Earl of

*Savers Gate is mentioned on old maps but no one seems to know where it was.

Harwich about 1700. The River Stour, top left, joins the River Orwell. Landguard Fort, right, guards the entry from the sea on the Felixstowe side of the estuary. *Essex Record Office*

Warwick, Lord Lieutenant of England, asked for nineteen guns for Harwich with powder and shot.

A map of 1534 shows where the walls and gates to the east with a tower, the remains of the castle, stood. The town gate lay at the south stretch of the walls. St Helen's Gate stood near the Green at the High Lighthouse end of King's Quay Street. A larger town gate opened its doors where the High Lighthouse now straddles the ancient site.

Along King's Quay Street today are many remains of old buildings with much to be done in the way of restoration. Three splendid Georgian houses, once owned by wealthy sea captains, stand at the southern end of the street near where St Helen's Gate had been built in former times. The later Victorian coal cellar of the first house is a hole made in the old town wall. The centre house was found to be of some extra interest when, in the 1940's, a wooden addition at the back was discovered to contain two hidden rooms. These rooms, one on top of the other, could be reached from the basement of Number 32, the third house. Perhaps men hid here from the press gangs.

Beside these houses is a minute quarter-house. It is tall with three floors, the same as its grander neighbours but it is so narrow it cannot even be said to be half a house, hence the term quarter-house. This house, Number 28, is an infill of 1830, being formerly the stable entrance for Number 30. Built on to it are picturesque cottages, white lattice on the walls and a large brass ship's bell. They are Georgian fronted, on Elizabethan timber and plaster, with a passageway by the side to the *Hanover Inn*. It is in this alleyway that the stretch of old septaria wall is best seen. Visitors to Harwich are proudly shown the wall from the churchyard side, but seldom from this alley. Here it can be seen as a very strong defensive wall.

Beyond the green of the churchyard, on the line where the wall foundations must lie buried, are garages. On the other side of King's Quay Street is the Electric Palace, a picture house built in 1911. The Electric Palace Trust intend to restore this cinema, which lies a few feet from the direct line of the wall, and is one of the earliest purpose built cinemas in Britain.

At right angles to the main street of Old Harwich lies Market Street, narrow and with small shops and houses. At the King's Quay end of the street once stood Burton's Gate but who or what was the Burton of the gate's name? The Harwich Society, whose interest and hard work has preserved much of old Harwich, will I hope one day mark all the gate sites with plaques similar to the ones Yarmouth has used. The next street, St Austen's Lane is where St Austen's Gate gave access through the eastern wall.

Castle Gate Street tells us that once a small gate led from the castle into the town. The castle itself stood near the present entrance to Navyard Wharf. At one time the great tower of the castle housed the town gaol.

On the next corner is the *Angel* public house, built in the nineteenth century. Not far from here, on old maps, on part of the Esplanade, is the word Angelgate. Was there an Angelgate let into the walls, from which the present *Angel* takes its name, or did the gate take it name from an earlier hostelry? Angelgate stands beside Outpart Eastward, shown on old maps, where once pillory, lock-up and the town ducking stool were known to have existed. There were cottages built for coastguards in 1858 at the old Angelgate, and the name is still remembered in the Redoubt. To quote the Harwich Society booklet on the Redoubt, "a gun battery of this name stood next to the present Customs Lookout at the time when the Redoubt was built."

At the far end of King's Quay Street, is East Gate Street, which further in the town joins St Austen's Lane at right angles. Here there must have been a gate facing the sea, otherwise why the name?

In 1665, Sir William Bolten obtained a patent from the King to erect lighthouses. Two were set up, one over the town gate, and the other, a low light at the edge of the Green.

One of the most exciting features of Harwich is the nineteenth century High Lighthouse, which stands 90 feet high at the edge of the old town. Old prints show several earlier wooden lighthouses which this one replaces. The present building was erected in 1818 and belonged to a General who became rich by exacting light tolls on ships coming into harbour. He charged 1d per ton. By 1863 the course of the channel had changed and the lighthouse became redundant. On the other side of the green beside the water the Low Lighthouse stands 45 feet high. This latter is ten-sided while the High Lighthouse has nine sides, an unusual number. When the lighthouses were in use together, the entrance was indicated when one light was vertically in line with the other, the reason for the differing heights of the lighthouses.

The High Lighthouse is built over the site of the old town gate. Some years ago this splendid building was sold for £75 and has been a private residence ever since. The Harwich Society have been involved with restoring the exterior of the lighthouse and a low cobbled circular wall has been built around the base, and the surrounding paths have been levelled.

In 1625 Harwich feared attacks by Dunkirkers and the Council ordered the county to defend the town. At that time each shire was expected to provide men for its own defence, but the crown was expected to build the defences and was bound to repay the costs of defence. More often than not the crown failed in its part of the bargain. In this case the men were ready long before the

The Harwich Redoubt being restored. A-The Lower and Upper Levels. B-Upper Level showing entrances to gun emplacements. C-Cannon found in the moat after cleaning and painting. D-Interior Lower Level room during repairs.

(A)

(B)

(C)

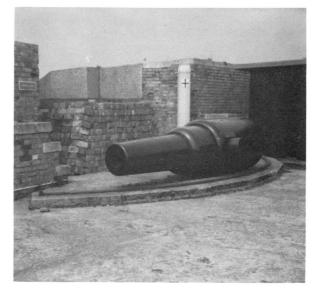

(D)

defences were supplied. Harwich forts were decayed, the platforms useless, so that there were 3,000 men with no ammunition at a time when strong naval power was essential. Trade and agriculture no longer existed under the threat of war and Harwich lived in this state for two years.

On the former Queen's Mount, erected in the reign of Queen Mary and where the Treadwheel Crane now stands, another fortification was erected. This fortification, then known as Dunn Bulwarke, consisted of a parapet round the mount of some thirty rods, fifteen feet high, thick at ground levels, four feet high and eleven feet thick at the top. The palisades before the entrance to the gate were forty-eight feet in length and seven feet high whilst those next to the tower were thirty feet long and seven feet high. There was also a guard court, a storehouse and a room with a chimney for the parapet sentry.

In 1666, during the Second Anglo-Dutch War, seventeen ships damaged in a four day naval battle came into Harwich for repairs. When the ships were ready some eight hundred men had deserted because of the horrors of plague deaths and war wounded dying in the streets.

Sir Bernard de Gomme was sent to Harwich in 1667 to inspect and advise on the state of the fortifications. A house crane, so called because it was enclosed in a building, was built, probably the one now standing on Harwich Green, to help with the defence of the town. Treadwheel cranes were common in England during the seventeenth century. At the end of that century however the power was taken over by donkeys.

In 1808 the Redoubt was built by French prisoners. This defended Harwich harbour with ten 24-pounder guns. Five more were placed south of the Redoubt and five on Beacon Cliff and a further five at the Angelgate. This Martello Tower is the largest on the coast and occupies a strategic position overlooking the approaches to Harwich. These towers, 103 of which were built from Seaford, Sussex to Aldeburgh, Suffolk, were smaller circular forts with massive walls. Built to guard against invasion by Napoleon, their name is a corruption of Cape Mortella in Corsica where a tower of this kind was captured by the English fleet in 1794.

Known as the Redoubt in Harwich, the Martello Tower is in a huge crater scooped out of the summit of a natural hill. A brick retaining wall, thirty feet deep, encircled the redoubt, making a dry moat and the outside of this was ramparted with earth. A drawbridge or retractable ladder over the moat afforded the only entry. It took three years to complete at the enormous cost of some £55,000.

Built in a vast circle round an inner courtyard 100 feet across, the walls were eight feet across with a parapet several feet thick to protect the men from the shot of the besieging force. Several stairways descended through the brickwork into the interior, which was honeycombed with large vaulted single-storey compartments for troops, ammunition and stores, sufficient to withstand a lengthy siege.

The rooms on both levels have been named, many with plaques above the door, by the Harwich Society, which is presently restoring the Redoubt. Lindsey (1) named after a nineteenth century architect and historian, was formerly the Canteen. Bigod (2), Lord of the Manor in the twelfth century was a soldiers' room, Dale (3) the Magazine after another historian. Hankyn (4) for the first Mayor of Harwich was the Artillery General Store, and Cann (5) after barge builders of the nineteenth century, was formerly a soldiers' room. The cookhouse now De Vere (6) named for the First Lord of the Manor who lived at Castle Hedingham. Fryatt (7) was the captain of a railway steamer which rammed a U-boat in 1915, and was shot by the Germans. The Hospital (8) is named for Carlyon Hughes a local historian, and Friese Greene (9) the inventor of cinematography who lived in Harwich, names another soldiers' room. Number (10) Garland, a former Lord of the Manor is the name over the library door, and Bagshaw (11) M.P. for Harwich in the nineteenth century has his name over the latrines and the coal store. Pepys (12) seventeenth century M.P. for Harwich is the name for the ablutions room. Deane (13) a master shipwright for a soldiers' room; Sally Port (14) a small door, the Guard Room; Pattrick (15) a local cement manufacturer, the shell store; Groom (16) shipowner, the Cells; Rebow (17) who inherited the High and Low Lighthouses and made a fortune, a soldiers' room; and Jones (18) Captain of the *Mayflower*, the name for the laboratory and cartridge store. These all on the lower level.

On the upper level the names given are Angel Gate (A) for a gun position; Nile Street (B), Hope Place (C), Cook Street (D), Box Street (E), King Street (F), Queen Street (G), Yeo Street (H), Tate Road (J), Bathside (K), many of which are not local names. They could have been named by the gun crews from their home areas.

High Ward (I) a family name, for an ammunition store, High Parkes (IV), High Abdy (VI) and High Vaux all for ammunition stores. Sally Port Stairs (II), Jones Stairs (V), De Vere Stairs (VIII), staircases. High Paine, an unknown who had an oak tree used as a sea mark (III), and High Pett (VII), the famous seventeenth century shipbuilders, both formerly shelters. A great deal of thought has gone into the naming of the rooms, staircases and parts of this Redoubt, to bring home to visitors and locals alike the vast history and tremendous number of notable people connected with Harwich throughout the ages.

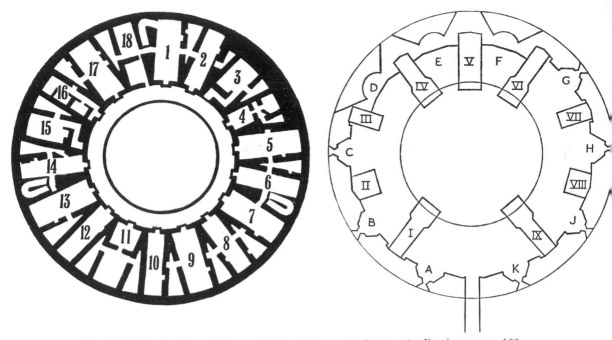

Harwich Redoubt Plans of Lower (left) and Upper (right) Levels. Key is on page 103.
Courtesy, The Harwich Society

The Redoubt continued to be occupied by the military until the First World War, when it fell into decay. Harwich Council bought the site in 1930 for housing purposes. New houses and gardens run right up to the moat, along with allotments. During the Second World War it came under the military authority for housing P.O.Ws.

In 1968 land hungry developers approached the council with a view to erecting houses or flats on the site, but it was on the list of Ancient Monuments, though no money was available for its repair. In 1969 a Harwich Society was formed to research the past and safeguard the future of Harwich, including its Martello Tower. With voluntary labour the Redoubt was done up and finally the Department of the Environment offered to pay half the cost. When the Society cleared the moat and centre of the Redoubt of the rubbish that had accumulated over the years of neglect a twelve ton cannon was found in the moat. This has now been placed in the Angel Gate embrasure. The Redoubt will become a museum when restoration is complete.

Harwich, like most east coast towns, has suffered unmercifully at the hands of the sea from flooding and coastal erosion, throughout its history. The town has always given valuable support to the nation in time of war. Always a principal port of exit and entry to and from Europe today, with adjacent

Parkeston, with which its name is constantly linked, Harwich watches Felixstowe, opposite across the River, in the battle for trade and passengers between Britain and the Continent.

*   *   *   *   *   *

Tilbury

Some two thousand years B.C., at the beginning of the New Stone Age, people becoming adventurous began to move away from their tribal homes. Sailing from the Spanish Peninsula, Portugal and France, in their dugout canoes, the Iberians moved up the west coast of England, Wales, Scotland and the east coast of Ireland. They came in search of land, minerals and precious stones and brought with them new arts: building, pottery, agriculture, polished stone weapons, spinning and weaving.

Further waves of invaders swept across the stretch of sea dividing Britain from the continent, coming from near the mouth of the Rhine from 1900 B.C. onwards. They landed on what is now the east Kent coast, while other invaders landed in the Wash — the first invaders to set foot on East Anglian shores. The natives of these shores put up some kind of defence but what form it took we do not know.

Between 700-400 B.C., the first Iron Age invaders came, again from the Rhine, and sailed up the Thames estuary, making their first contact with Essex. Later they built hill forts in their new living areas because of a threat of a new wave of Iron Age invaders who arrived from 400-150 B.C. and came from the Seine-Marne area, the Marnians. There are many Iron Age finds giving proof of these early invasions.

During the second century B.C. the Belgae of mixed Teuton and Celtic blood from north east France and Belgium arrived in Britain. These early Belgae were then called Catuvellaunians and spread across the Thames making a capital first at Wheathampstead, later at Prewood, St Albans, then, in A.D. 10, at Colchester, abandoning forever the hillforts and settlements on lower ground. They had kings, their own coins and organised states, and kept a high standard of living in what was still prehistoric Britain. They imported goods from Rome and produced a surplus of goods, including slaves, which they traded with the Roman Empire. This was indeed the reason Claudius sent a probing expedition to Britain in 55 B.C., with an eye to later conquest. Obviously Britain would be a desirable acquisition to the Roman Empire.

The *Anglo-Saxon Chronicle* mentions Tiliberia, and the Domesday Book that the area was held by Alvric a freeman priest, in the time of King Edward the Confessor. There was pasture for 300 sheep and a fishery; 9 swine, 31 beasts (animalia) and 12 colts; 4 hides of woodland; 1 villein, 11 borders and 2 serfs.

The Essex shore of the Thames was extensively inhabited by the Romans as finds, over the years, have indicated, and there was a Roman settlement at West Tilbury. The number of Roman finds at the site of the ancient ferry in 1872 exceeds the number often found at recognised Roman forts although no fort is known to have existed at that place. There is known to have been a Roman salt-making industry east of where the present fort stands, as well as Roman villas and other buildings.

The first known defences, on the banks of the River Thames, were earthworks and blockhouses, wooden defence towers or bretasks. These blockhouses virtually defended the city of London, if only from a distance, therefore for the purposes of this book they can be mentioned as being town or city defences and they certainly had walls of a sort. Fourteenth and fifteenth century temporary blockhouses guarded the Gravesend-Tilbury ferry crossing, but by the sixteenth century they had become obsolete.

Five artillery blockhouses were sited on the Thames banks at Higham, Milton and Gravesend on the Kent side, and at East and West Tilbury on the Essex side, to prevent attack on London by enemy ships. These two-storied structures were "D" shaped with the straight side facing inland, but no traces remain today.

Henry VIII developed a national plan of coastal defences in 1539, building forts as strategic sites on coasts and river banks. One of the most important of these was the one built over the site of the old blockhouse at West Tilbury. The blockhouse survived much altered, inside the later Tilbury Fort throughout three hundred years. The defence was altered during the Armada scare of mid July 1588, to add to its strength.

Four thousand soldiers were gathered at Tilbury Fort in 1588 under the Earl of Leicester, Commander in Chief of Queen Elizabeth's troops. These men were brought together from all over the country and many were billeted within the fort. The Queen wanted to lead the troops against the Spanish Armada, but this Leicester refused to allow. Nevertheless she encouraged her troops saying that, "though she had but the body of a weak and feeble woman, she had the heart of a king, and of a king of England too." When the Armada was driven off the danger remained and additional work to the fort was carried out. A timber drawbridge was constructed, gates were renewed, and a palisading of 1,500 fir poles erected. Men dug an outer ditch and threw up

Tilbury Fort, a reconstruction of how it might have looked about 1725, drawn by Alan Sorrell.
Crown Copyright

counterscarp banks. Finally chains, cables and ships' masts were formed into an enormous boom. This river defence was anchored to lighters on either side of the water.

The fort was somewhat neglected during the early seventeenth century although the garrison was maintained. Indeed the outer earthworks were in such poor repair that during high tides the Thames flowed into the fort, and both cattle and people strayed inside. Charles II when in exile had seen permanent fortifications abroad and realized their immense strategic value and on his restoration to the throne mounted a national campaign of defence. Sir Bernard de Gomme became Chief Engineer in 1666 and produced several plans for a new fort. Finally in 1670 work begun on the regular pentagonal fort which still stands beside the Thames at Tilbury today.

1671 saw a special warrant issued that men be impressed to work at the fort. This meant that work had to be done, and goods had to be sold to the

Crown at prices lower than the current value. Workmen were pressed into service from villages in Essex and Kent, one impressment alone being responsible for the enforced labour of 250 men. Skilled carpenters and stone-masons however came from local builders. Two new moats were cut and the ground level raised to eliminate flooding, while the ancient ditches were filled with earth from the old Elizabethan ramparts. Ships from Norway brought piles for all buildings inside the fort as well as the bastions and curtain walls, because of the marshy nature of the riverside site. Ten years later the fort was armed although covered ways between moats had still not been built, palisades were incomplete, sentry boxes were not yet in existence, and two gates and much of the brickwork remained to be completed. The fort was finally finished in 1683 but eleven years later guns were sinking into the ground throwing shot in the air because of rotten timber platforms which were then replaced in stone.

Powder magazines were built on both sides of the Landport Gate in 1716 and new barracks for officers and soldiers some fifty years later. Towards the end of the century it was realized the chief fault with the fort was the lack of a water bastion, near the Water Gate on the river, the area being virtually undefended. The Water Bastion was begun but never completed, instead a six-gun battery was built at the south-east corner of the covered way, giving an excellent line of fire down river. Repairs and alterations were made at Tilbury over the years, to keep up with the latest ideas of defence. This continued until the First World War, when the south-east battery was mounted with improved weapons. During the Second World War a Gun Operations Room in the

The Officers Barracks, Tilbury, with the Queen Anne guns beside the parade ground.

chapel controlled anti-aircraft defences until a new building was ready at Vange.

The most incredible thing about this massive fort however is the fact that it was never used for its original purpose.

One man, Edward Lawrence, is said to have saved Tilbury Fort from 700 attacking Irishmen, but no one seems to know how the fort was saved, nor why the Irish were there. In 1776, during a cricket match between Essex and Kent, a player from Kent shot and killed an Essex cricketer. The players on both sides armed themselves and as a result the sergeant in charge of the fort and an elderly invalid soldier died. The cricketers scattered, Kentishmen across the river and men of Essex over the drawbridge. During the First World War a German Zeppelin was shot down by anti-aircraft guns at the fort. During the Second World War soldiers were barracked in temporary quarters but these were blown down. An enemy plane was shot down by the fort's anti-aircraft guns.

The entrance to the fort was once via the redan in the north. Here a redoubt, built by de Gomme, stood to defend the road entrance. A causeway led to the covered-way between the moats and the fort itself. A ravelin island in the inner moat was an added point of defence opposite Landport Gate, and served as a check point of entry to the fort. Its guns could cover the northward-lying land, and it was linked to the covered-way by timber draw-bridges. Sluices controlled the water level of the moats. They were a means of keeping the moats clean and were an added defence, because they could be emptied of water, particularly in times of hard frost, to prevent the moats becoming frozen over and an enemy approaching across the ice.

The Landport Gate was the final place of entry to the fort after one had traversed the surrounding country to the north, the redan, the causeway, ravelin, drawbridge and covered-way. This gate led to the barracks, parade ground, magazines, gun emplacements, guard room and chapel.

This fort with preserved covered-ways, moats and rampart is acknowledged to be the finest example of military engineering of the period in which it was built, its complexity and size comparing favourably with similar continental forts.

In 1950 the War Department handed the fort over to the Ministry of Works* as a national monument, and now Tilbury Fort is a splendid part of our national heritage, easily accessible to the public.

Twentieth century visitors enter the fort by the very fine ashlar faced Water Gate, decorated with Ionic columns and bas-relief trophies of arms. An inscription over the entrance reads, "CAROLUS II REX. AO. REG. XXXIV."

*Now Department of the Environment.

This Water Gate stands behind the quay and causeway from which munitions and stores were brought into the fort. At low tide the original piles, a foot in diameter, can be seen, the remains of the unfinished Water Bastion. Buildings next to the Water Gate house a small but excellent museum. In the two powder magazines considerable care has always been taken against accidental ignition of gun powder and no nails were used in the building, only wooden pegs to avoid sparks. The doors to the south are covered with sheets of copper as a protection against fire. The magazines have the additional protection of blast walls on three sides.

Over the Landport Gate there is a rectangular room, the gatehouse or Dead House. Stories are told of prisoners hung here and their bodies being dropped through a trap-door in the floor into carts waiting below. Certainly there is a trapdoor in this darkly shuttered room. During the Jacobite Rebellion of 1745, 380 Scottish rebels are said to have died, their bodies taken via the trapdoor, across the drawbridge, but their burial place has never been found. One story of the time states that spectators were allowed, at a charge of six pence, to see the prisoners and to spit on them. There are paintings on the wall said to have been painted in the prisoners' own blood.

Stone gun emplacements at Tilbury.

6. The South East

IPSWICH — COLCHESTER

Ipswich

IPSWICH, situated where the Gipping discharges into the Orwell, is an important East Anglian town. Suburbs surround the town, and the centre has the usual modern shops, multi-storied car parks, but very little that is old has remained for posterity.

Permanent settlement of the site was unknown before middle Saxon times but Prehistoric and Roman sites exist within the present borough boundary. The existence of a castle is known, but what happened in the castle is not. Indeed historical fact about Ipswich defences is somewhat sparse.

Ipswich was a town of some importance in the second half of the tenth century because coins have been found from the reign of Edgar, 964 the earliest extant, to the reign of Henry III, struck at an Ipswich mint. Only important towns were permitted to have mints. The Saxon coins were found in the centre of the town somewhere in the right angle between Upper Brook Street and Tacket Street.

The Danes sailed up the River Orwell, landed a body of men, sacked the town and retired before an adequate force could be brought against the invaders. Ipswich was surrounded by a rampart defended on the outside by a ditch but this was broken down by the Danes who pillaged the town in 991 and 1000.

During the wars with the Danes several strong places of defence were built. It is not known if William I surrounded the town with a ditch and wall after their demolition by the Danes. It has however been suggested that the Ipswich Castle was built by the Conqueror and destroyed during the reign of Henry II. Archaeological evidence suggests that the town was protected only by a ditch and an earthen bank, first cut in the eleventh

111

century, beneath the line of the later rampart, which was constructed in the early thirteenth century. The ditch was re-cut later in the thirteenth century, and before the end of its life had inserted, on its line, a trench with vertical sides, perhaps a foundation trench for a stone wall that was never completed. If this is indeed the case, it might be linked with the licence to crenellate issued in 1352 and abandoned two years later when the ditch was filled in.

In 1299 the town obtained a grant of murage from the Crown for five years. That they intended to build a stone wall is indicated by a grant to Robert Jolyff of a piece of ground in the town common ditches for the purpose of erecting dye-works, unless a stone wall was erected there to enclose the town. There is no evidence that the wall was erected and the Crown grant may have been used to recut the ditch. The ditch was a modification of a stream bed which ran from high ground outside the town and formed the eastern boundary known to this day as The Wash.

The defensive ditch was irregular, broad, U-shaped, and ran from the west, and apparently, turned a broad corner to the west. The ditch was very close to the site of the later line of the town defence but not aligned to it.

There is no documentary evidence to prove that Ipswich ever had a stone defensive wall, nor conclusive evidence of a rampart and ditch before 1204. However pottery and the mint show the town was important throughout Saxon times. Domesday says it had a minster church and these churches only occurred in important towns. Domesday also shows Ipswich to be in decay, so its heyday was over.

The earliest account of these defences are found in the time of John in 1203, "the king caused the Ditch and Wall to be made by the aide of the county and of the county of Cambridge." It was not unusual for distant towns and counties to be charged for aid for the defence of other places.

In 1346 the Friars were granted the privilege of acquiring a void place in the dyke 100 feet square from John Harnes provided the Bailiffs and Commonalty were allowed free ingress to repair the walls for defence in time of war or when necessary. The Court Pipe Rolls inform us that during 1434 John Frede had a "Common Soile, parcel of the Towne Ditche at the Barr Gates, at 6d rent." Peter Joy had a "parcel of Common Soile by way, nigh Towne Ditche, over against the way from the round crosse to Blackfriars Bridge," in 1479.

A manuscript of 1592 proves that the Ditch and Wall followed the line of what is Lady Lane. The walls and ditch against the almshouses in Lady Lane

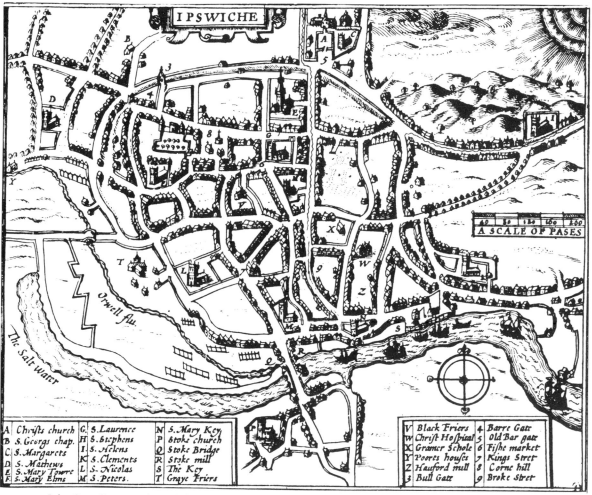

A	Chrifts church	G.	S. Laurence	N	S. Mary Key
B	S. Georgs chap.	H	S. Stephens	P	Stoke church
C.	S. Margarets	I.	S. Helens	Q	Stoke Bridge
D.	S. Mathews	K.	S. Clements	R	Stoke mill
E.	S. Mary Towre	L.	S. Nicolas	S	The Key
F.	S. Mary Elms	M.	S. Peters.	T	Graye Friers

V	Black Friers	4	Barre Gatt
W	Chrift Hoſpital	5	Old Bar gate
X	Gramer Schole	6	Fiſhe market
Y	Poores houſes	7	Kings Strett
Z	Hauford mill	8	Corne hill
3	Bull Gatt	9	Broke Strett

John Speed's map of Ipswich, 1610, shows the course of the defences when portions of the bank were extant and probably the ditch was not filled in in places.

were then "dooled out." A defensive tower was raised sometime in the late twelfth or early thirteenth century, giving its name to St Mary's church which was later built on the south side of the old tower. It appears this tower was already in existence before the year 1204 when the wall and ditches were constructed.

John Speed's map of 1610, the earliest map of Ipswich, shows the course of the defences, when portions of the bank were extant and probably the ditch was not filled in in places. Later maps preserve, even to the present day, the helmet shape of the defences in the road pattern. No sign of these defences exist today except for the rise in the ground at Tower Ramparts.

Tower Ramparts is a name which conjures up the past, bringing with it visions of crenellated towers and huge ramparts. A photograph taken at the beginning of this century shows part of the rampart still raised in the middle of the street. Now the sharp curve of this part of former defence remains only as a slight slope in the new road. Further along to the east however Tower Ramparts comes into its own with buildings that come straight out of medieval times. South of Tower Ramparts by Tower Street the whole of Ipswich appears to be sliding downhill following the direction the rampart took.

The rampart was excavated by the Ministry of Works in 1959, when Tollemaches Brewery bought the remaining fragment of the defence. It appears that one end of the rampart still stood eight feet high, the ditch itself originally being five feet deep and twenty feet wide, the ground falling away to a stream bed. This was the rampart constructed in 1204. Later work on the rampart and ditch destroyed all traces of the early wooden palisading.

Inside where Tower Ramparts meets Northgate, the roads are old, narrow and medieval. Northgate, outside, again there is the contrast of old and new, in those early buildings of old Ipswich.

Documentary evidence tells of a licence to strengthen and crenellate in 1352. A stone wall was built along the outer face of the rampart wall three feet thick, the lower courses faced with blocks of septaria, above flint cobbles, used with occasional binding slabs of larger material. A small vertical sided ditch was dug for foundations of a wall, but the project was abandoned and filled in soon after. The original earth bank and ditch continued to suffice until the seventeenth century and only the gates ever acquired pretensions.

A document of 1553 says, "The town Walls and Ditches shall be cast up and repaired by the inhabitants that have any ground adjoining to the walls and ditches before Easter next" and that turnpikes were to be set up before that time. This refers to an intention to put the town in a defensive position on the accession of Mary. One might think that from the use of the word wall, that it would have been of stone but this was not so as only an earthen wall served Ipswich.

On a portion of the wall, anciently on the north side of the church of St Mary at the Tower, now St Mary le Tower, stood a defensive tower which gave its name to the church and Tower Street. The existence of this tower seems to prove that the town had been surrounded by a defensive wall before the period of King John, when the ditch and walls were made.

In 1603 James I agreed, "That the wall ditches of the towne shalbe inclosed with palls and gates and styles, att the endes thereof; and that the ditche shalbe cast upp and gravelled above and that the chardges thereof shalbe bore as follows — first the one halfe of the castings upp of the same Ditch and the palings shalbe borne att the church of the towne; and the gate and the rest of the church to be borne by those that have ground on eyther side of the said Ditch, and that they have back gates to their groundes shall have keyes to such gates as shalbe made for the inclosing thereof."

The walls and ditches were repaired for the last time during the Civil War. A letter to the Bailiff, dated 1643, said that the ditches about the town were badly decayed and trodden down and that horses had been ridden up and down upon them, "and I feare they are much digged down where men have private yards against them." A court order was made that the ramparts should be "metered with palles and the gates at the end there of, and that the Ditch be shall cast up and gravelled above." Extensive repairs cost £326 and a further £10 for 10 iron cannon, especially imported from London, for the defence of the town, was expended.

In 1618 it was agreed that the wall ditch on the south end of the goal was to be referred to the headburrows to be let as they thought right. The wall was repaired again during the Civil War in 1643. At the close of the seventeenth century the bank was heightened by three feet to provide a wide, flat platform. An assembly of 1643 gave orders for making breastworks and fortifications around the town on the advice of the bailiffs and the deputy lieutenants or who ever they cared to consult. The treasurer was to provide, immediately, fifty or sixty broad or hand barrows and baskets. The assembly said that orders had to be given to prevent passage over the town walls and for a watch to be kept by the petty constables by night and the headburrows by day.

Although there was never a stone wall at Ipswich, there were four stone gates. These were North Gate, also known as Old Bar Gate or St Margaret's Barr Gate, West Gate or Barre Gate, East Gate and South Gate. Little seems to be known of the North, South and East Gates and I know of no engravings which depict them but East Gate is marked on Speed's map.

A Bull Gate was built in Great Bolton Lane in 1603 and was not connected with the town walls as such. This gate was erected by a Mr Bull who leased land from the corporation on condition that he "bylde a gate house thereon". The East Gate is said to have been at the junction of Fore Street and St Clement's South Gate to have been opposite where Wolsey's Gateway stands in Key Street near St Peter's church.

North Gate is ancient but no one knows when it was built. At the end of its life it so obstructed the highway that when the Paving and Lighting Commission obtained the powers of their Act in 1793, the first thing they did was to demolish the old gate. The stones from the gate may still be seen at the *Halberd Inn* in Northgate Street. Strangely enough, George Frost, who lived in Ipswich prior to the demolition of North Gate, although he sketched many of the town's antiquities, left no traceable record of this gate. The West Gate, unlike the other gates, is referred to in records but sadly no trace of this lovely edifice now remains. It was demolished in 1782.

When a sewer was laid in Westgate Street, the massive foundations of the old gateway which stood across St Matthew's Street were found. Two prints of the gate, one from the inside and another from the outside, make an interesting contrast. The west front had two projecting bastion-like multiangular towers which make the gate seem immense, while the east front shows only a decorated flat facade and, although two-storied, the whole appears to be minute.

The lower part of the west front was stone, while the upper was faced, at a later period, with local red brick, the two floors being separated by a bold projecting string course of stone. The red brick upper storey was somewhat deeper than the lower storey, no doubt adding to its impressive appearance. Slightly off centre a square wooden town clock dial projected over the centrally placed heavily barred window in the upper chamber and the central carriageway arch. The whole of this front was asymmetrical and gained in artistic quality and beauty as a result. The clock had but one hand, a sign of its antiquity.

Tower Ramparts, Ipswich, about 1904. *Photographer unknown*

The clock itself has more recorded history than all the other three gates put together, and that is just the clock, not the West Gate. It was a Town Clock, set on a Town Gate, and Borough Gaol, even so the Citizens of Ipswich were responsible for its upkeep. The records at St Matthew's Church state:

"1629 Whereof in Mr. Hayles hands wch is agreed to be allowed him towards his charges oute about the fynishinge of ye clock in the Borogate, xis. More agreed to be paid to Baddston for keeping the new clock iij quarters of a year xiijs. iiijd.*

1630 Whereof they are to pay to the sexton for keepinge of the clock one whole yeare, ended at Easter last. xiiis. iiijd.

1704. To Roger Moore, for clening and mending ye Goale Clock 1s. 6d.

1777. Oct.7th Oil the Clock 1s. 0d.

1778. April 19th. For a Clock Line. 1s. 6d.

1780. April 14th. Thos.Read, for a Clock Line. 2s. 6d."

The Memorial Book of the church has an entry:

"1698. Memorandum that there is a note in the Church Chart under the hand of Roger Moore, which oblige him to keepe the Goal Clock in good repaire during his life for eighteen pence a year."

An even later addition in deeper red brick was the over-sailing course, carried on dwarf blind arcades, and capped with a coped battlement, across the central part of the gate and along one angle on either side of the flanking bastion towers. At the angle corners, where they meet the blind arcading, parapets projected, with apertures supported by arches. These overhanging parapets prevented assailants creeping up unnoticed, and rendered attempts to scale the towers impossible.

But this defensive strength and ornamentation lay only on the west front of the gate. In the left hand tower beside the tower door there was a lancet-headed window, and three windows in the upper storey. This facade had pointed gables and the tiled roofs covered in the archway and towers, the roofs themselves being visible from the west front. The east front was coursed ashlar masonry, which at one time was covered with plaster. From the middle of the centre roof a wooden framework bell turret rose, with a steeply pitched roof of tiles, surmounted by a knob finial and a banner vane. Off centre in the middle gable was another clock.

There were apertures through which boiling oil or molten lead could be poured on the heads of assailants. The right hand tower had a cruciform loop-hole for use with arrows and bullets and although the parapets might look highly decorative they were in fact built for defensive use. Whether the defensive strength of the gate was ever used to the full we do not know. The lower part of the gate is said to be of the period of about 1370, while the upper storey was built some hundred years later.

*j was the final form of i in Latin thus xiijs. iiijd. is 13s. 4d.

During the reign of Henry VI, John de Caldwell built a common gaol at the Barre Gate. Gaol entries were recorded until the end of the eighteenth century although the West Gate Gaol fell out of use long before that time. In 1652 pirates were confined in the prison, so its security was in no doubt. Foreign prisoners were lodged there waiting exchange. Long after the West Gate fell into disuse escapees used to be lodged in a cell in a tower of the Gate, this being no more than a dungeon black hole. The borough gaol at that time was merely two town houses with large gardens.

Later still the tower upper rooms were used as gunpowder stores, while the lower floor was used to confine soldiers and house the guard. During the eighteenth century the gate was offered for sale. At a Great Court of 17th November, 1781 it was agreed that St Matthew's Gate, built in 1430, be sold to the highest bidder, so that it could be pulled down. The *Ipswich Journal* of 15th December 1781 reported "Saturday last the West Gate in this town was sold to be pulled down, for £32." In July, 1782 the Corporation, "Agreed and ordered that a lease for 99 years be made of so much of the piece of waste ground at St Matthew's Gate to Mr John Cobbold, as adjoin to and abuts upon his premises called 'The Feathers', at a yearly rent of one shilling." So nearly two hundred years ago this lovely gate fell to the demolition gang of the day.

*　　*　　*　　*　　*　　*

Colchester

Cunobelinus, the most famous king of the Belgic tribes of Britain, once lived in Camulodunum. Today we know Camulodunum as Colchester, and that the Belgae were people of mixed origin, Celts and Teutons from the lower Rhine.

The town was defended by banks and ditches, known as dykes, which, by their very height and depth, were excellent defence against chariots and cavalry. The nearest dykes were half a mile away at Sheepen, others further out.

Colchester became a Roman fortress, after the Belgae had left the area. This fortress is thought to have been situated in the western half of the present town, probably bounded by North Hill, Head Street, Vineyard Street and Nunn's Road. Recent excavations at Lion Walk and elsewhere confirm the fortress idea. Defensive ditches and ramparts were found as well as several military buildings. The Romans invaded Britain in A.D. 43 and Colchester was founded as a colonia in about A.D. 49. We know that Boadicea burnt London, St Albans and Colchester in A.D. 60 or 61, and that military buildings at Lion Walk were razed during this revolt.

A wall section, between two shops on North Hill, Colchester, marks the place near which the North Gate once stood.

This colonia at Camulodunum was supported by a strong body of veterans. These old soldiers called the Iceni slaves and captives, treated them cruelly and drove them from their own lands. The common Roman soldiers followed the veteran tyranny with licentious behaviour.

The Saxon raiders harassed Colchester during the third, fourth and fifth centuries. So much so that further defensive ditches were dug round the town, leaving gaps for the roads leading from the main gates. Finally for extra defence a ditch was dug across the front of the Balkerne Gate and traffic diverted to the Head Gate.

The Danes occupied Colchester in the tenth century and the *Anglo-Saxon Chronicle* tells us that Edward the Elder (901-924) is said to have repaired parts of the town walls which lay in ruins after the earlier Danish invasion.

The late Saxons lived mainly within the walls of Colchester, building their own roads, leaving only the main streets of Roman Colchester as they were in their original positions, namely Head Street, Queen Street and North Hill Street.

After the Norman Conquest the walls became the responsibility of the town authorities. During the reign of Edward III, several persons were indicted for bearing off, or meddling with, the parapet stones, also digging pits near to the foundation. In Richard the Second's time the cost of repairing so large a structure, of keeping up the gates, fosse, and approaches, appears to have fallen heavily upon the townspeople, especially as they were otherwise heavily taxed; to relieve them, the King exempted the burgesses of Colchester from the cost of sending representatives to Parliament for three years.

Colchester walls are unique in Britain and were built probably in the first part of the second century A.D., of locally made tiles and septaria in rectangular blocks. The experts say the walls are all of the same period and were mostly eight and a half feet thick with a base three feet wider, and covered a circuit of one and a half miles. Two walls were built of septaria and brick courses having thick joints of mortar to give the septaria additional strength and these constituted the outside faces. The cavity between the two was filled with more septaria and mortar. The walls had rampart walks, parapets with widely spaced merlons, earthen ramparts behind and wide, deep ditches in front. The walls remained in use until the siege of 1648. Sometime after 1382, certainly during the next forty years, the walls were repaired and eight bastions were built on to the walls. Seven of these have been placed exactly by archaeologists and are marked on maps. The East Gate of Colchester was built by the Romans, but exactly when is not known.

In the Civil War the Parliamentary armies had better resources than the Royalists and by 1648 had imprisoned the King. Sir Charles Lucas, whose family mansion was in Colchester, raised a force of unemployed weavers of that town to fight for the king. They marched to Braintree on 10th June 1648 to enlarge their forces and seize more armoury, barrels of gun powder and other instruments of war. Returning to Colchester with his troops to the gates of the town, Lucas found them shut as he knew they would be and the Royalists not welcome. Outside sixty armed horsemen with scouts were on guard at the turnpike. A scout was shot and the people of Colchester decided to let the troops in, bargaining that in return for entrance, the inhabitants were to be left unmolested and the town unplundered.

Lord Goring and Sir Charles Lucas, intending to stay only a night or two in the town before marching north to recruit more men, entered with some five or six thousand troops, a third of which were well armed, and four hundred cavalry. General Fairfax, at the head of the Parliamentary army, arrived in Colchester and demanded immediate surrender.

That afternoon Fairfax's soldiers attacked both Head and Schere Gate; getting so near to the former as to be able to fire under it and to throw stones over the top.

Fairfax, determined to hem the Royalists in, began building a fort on the London Road which was called Fort Essex. He also seized Mersea Fort to stop supplies reaching Colchester. The army inside built a fort in St Mary's churchyard, in the south west corner of the Roman town. They knew a long siege had begun so they set about collecting supplies. Enormous stores of fish, wine, corn and gun powder were brought from the Hythe into the town. Men were detailed to rampart the walls inside and the Balkerne Gate was converted into an artillery bastion. All townsmen of between sixteen and sixty were conscripted into the Royalist Army, but being pressed men were of little use. Fairfax, too, increased his forces from the surrounding towns of the eastern counties.

Messages went back and forth between the two sides to put an end to the fighting, but no agreement was reached. Fairfax continued with his plans to encircle the town with forts, while the Royalists bombarded them with cannon fire from St Mary's churchyard. On the 5th July Fairfax took delivery of forty guns from the Tower of London, for his forts — the Royalists had only 20 guns.

Around midnight on 5th or 6th July the famous East Street Sortie took place. Sir Charles Lucas led two hundred cavalry, and Sir George Lisle five hundred foot soldiers, down the East Hill. Wading across the river and crossing the footbridge, they drove the enemy away from the garrison in the mill at East Bridge. But a Royalist soldier calling in the darkness for more ammunition, carelessly revealed how short they were of ammunition. The Roundheads renewed their attack and the Royalists retreated. Sorties and fighting went on night after night.

It was inevitable that the town would have to surrender as food became scarce. By the 18th July cheese and butter normally only a few pence, cost five shillings a pound, and the horses were killed for their meat, which was of poor quality as the horses were also starving. At night the soldiers often stripped thatch from rooftops to feed the poor beasts. Cats and dogs were also eaten and six shillings was paid for the side of a very small dog.

Finally the townspeople, having suffered and endured a siege of some fifty-nine days, demanded that the Royalist troops surrender. Every night they brought their women and screaming, starving children to Lord Goring's headquarters.

The Royalists, who were waiting for the best possible terms from the Roundheads, refused to give in. With no corn left, rye, peas, oats and barley had all in turn been used to make bread and over eight hundred horses had been eaten. On 23rd August a search throughout every house in the city revealed that only one day's food was left for the inhabitants.

Two days later the Royalists sent a message that they would open a gate for Fairfax, afterwards claiming they had not offered him entry. They

121

prepared barrels of boiling pitch and scythes with long handles but Fairfax made no move. Finally on the 28th August, 1648, 3,531 town men surrendered when only half a barrel of gun powder remained. Fairfax rode into the town and lost no time in having the Royalists executed. Lucas and Lisle were shot and of the soldiers taken prisoner many died in the country, others were transported as slaves to the West Indies. The walls of the town were breached on the orders of General Fairfax, so they would be of no further use to the town. Today Siege House, with its Civil War bullet holes, may still be seen near East Bridge.

The East Gate occupied only half of the width of the present road and in 1651 the gate fell down. The Chamberlain was allowed, out of the town revenues, six pounds to carry away the rubble of the East Gate to make the way passable for carts and horses and was allowed to keep the stones, lead and iron for his own use. The gate must have been repaired or rebuilt because 1675 records state: "East Gate is out of repair, and soe dangerous that it is believed that it will suddenly fall, whereby great mischief may be done." The gate is said to have had a central carriageway and a footway on either side.

Near the East Gate site is Bastion 1, added to the wall in the time of Richard II. The wall here is dilapidated and apparently repaired both with and without permission from the authorities. Here a car park hugs the wall from opposite St Botolph's Priory almost as far as East Gate.

Bastion V was thoroughly examined in 1931 because the Eastern National Omnibus Company granted excavators time to dig properly. The tower is round outside with a flat side against the wall, a typical D-plan tower like so

A plaque on the bastion wall at Colchester which records date of building, excavation, restoration and addition of a summer house.

A notice in a Colchester kitchen shop, "Mind your head on the Roman wall".

many East Anglian defensive towers. At the top are the remains of an eighteenth century summer house. The bus station and multi-storey car park have been built behind, inside, the wall on a higher level. Inside at this point the wall only rises some one and a half feet high above present ground level, outside the wall is much higher. A plaque attached to the Bastion wall dates the excavation.

> BASTION V
> LATE 14th CENTURY
> SUMMERHOUSE ADDED
> LATE 18th CENTURY
> EXCAVATED 1931
> RESTORED 1964.

Little is known about the South Gate, because the walls have been covered with buildings for so many years. Somewhere near Eld Lane, or at the end of Long Wyre Street, there may have been a South Gate. If so, the latter would have been a logical opposite to Rye Gate in the north wall. St Botolph's Gate is said to have stood in medieval times and indeed up to 1817, at the end of Queen Street, so it is possible this gate was built on the site of a former Roman gate. Sir Mortimer Wheeler says, about the road from Mersea, an important one, that it "should strike the town west of St Botolph's Gate, and opposite Rye Gate, but no record of such a gate is known." If such a gate existed, then it could be somewhere near the southern part of Long Wyre Street.

Until quite recently the wall from Long Wyre Street westwards was hidden by houses. These walls have now been revealed by a demolition and an enormous building project. Here is a new three-storey shopping precinct with an underground loading-bay. In one part of the wall someone with a sense of humour has a garage inside the wall. I must admit to hysterical indignation further west when I saw that a 26 feet wide hole had been knocked in one of the most famous walls in England, to allow passageway. "You can't get in the way of development," said a workman on the site accepting this authorised vandalism. Shops and flats rise on and above the ancient repaired Roman wall, and concrete steps stride over the past and down to the outside world. A few hundred yards to the east the remains of a bastion tower, in a narrow alley, facing towards Vine Street, stand alone. The top part of the tower is a room in a house which backs on to Eld Lane.

To the east is lovely Scheregate. Here is the site of the medieval Shere or Southcherd Gate, commemorated by the name of the narrow alley which leads up to narrow steps where the former gate stood. Local people are proud of it and almost everyone knows some of its history. The Roman town wall lies complete beneath Scheregate Steps, which proves that in Roman times no gate existed at this point. When the site was excavated in 1926, while a cable trench was being cut through the steps, the wall was found to be fourteen feet thick. If a Roman gate did exist, then it must be somewhere east of Scheregate.

Further to the west, set back from St John's Street, at number 48A, is Trader's Kitchen Shop. Shops such as this are a delight to many people, but this one is unique. Inside behind a wrought iron spiral staircase, is a notice which says, "MIND YOUR HEAD ON THE ROMAN WALL." A timely notice, if you would avoid a resultant headache as you proceed through that doorway-hole in the wall down into what is probably a Tudor cellar built on to the inside of the town wall. The cellar now houses earthenware, glassware and up to date kitchen equipment.

At the corner of Butt Road where it joins St John's Street, Head Street and Crouch Street, Head Gate is said to have stood in Roman times. Beyond this the south west corner of the Roman wall is non-existent, having been demolished on the orders of Fairfax during the siege.

The south west postern stands beside St Mary's-at-the-Wall churchyard. It has been called the postern near Colkyngs Castle or Castell. The church was destroyed probably at the same time as the south west corner of the wall. The postern was rebuilt after the siege with an enlarged passageway and steps down the outside of the wall. Immediately north of this postern there was a fort, built by the army. This jutted some six feet from the wall inside. St Mary's church, behind, was a Royalist stronghold and according to tradition had a one-eyed sharp-shooter stationed in the belfry. The belfry was damaged by gunfire, which also killed the sharp-shooter, and the church was gutted. The lower stages of the fifteenth century tower is all that remains of the original church and the belfry replaced in 1729. The present brick top was added in 1911.

In the early days the Balkerne Gate was known as Colkyngs Castle, from King Coel, or the Balcon, according to two conflicting theories. It may be that the name Balkerne came from the Old Saxon word balk (baulk), to beam, or the Old English word balca meaning a ridge between furrows. It was once the West Gate, the main gate of the town, which led to London and as such was of great importance. Originally the centre part of Balkerne Gate is said to have been built at a monumental arch, a *Portes Monumentales*, independent of walls and gates and possibly built to mark the original limits of the town, or to celebrate the finishing of the Roman road to St Albans and London. When the town was enclosed the gate was incorporated into the walls.

Work was begun on excavations in 1913 by H. Laver and E. N. Mason, but Mr. Mason died. In 1917 (Sir) R. E. M. Wheeler completed the excavation: the gate was found to be one hundred and seven feet long, north to south, and thirty-nine feet from back to front, thirty feet of which projected out of the west face of the wall.

The gate had two seventeen foot wide carriage-ways divided by a central pier and two pedestrian ways each six feet wide. On either side of the entrances were enormous towers each with a large quadrant shaped guardroom, leading from a passage. The gate foundations were of septaria and flint with sandy mortar. The core of the walls was the same with facing tiles of dressed volcanic rock blocks. It was a remarkable gate because it had four portals, which were at one period completely blocked in by a rough wall eight or nine feet thick, built across them. This wall was said to be a means of defence when the gate was in ruins; possibly built by the Saxons or Danes. The lowest part of the south tower and the barrel vaulting of its pedestrian way are still standing. *The Hole in the Wall* public house is built on the stump of the north tower of the gate.

The postern gate at St Mary's Steps is not Roman. The arch which was excavated was too low for a postern arch and was found to be a drain. In the sixteenth century this was enlarged to give access to Balkerne Lane.* This drain was part of a system of Roman drains built when the wall was made.

*The location of Balkerne Lane is now part of Balkerne Way.

The wall then drops steeply down Balkerne Hill to turn a typically rounded Roman corner. The wall here, inside the Gilberd School, has very little of its face showing. In most places the wall in the grounds is reveted to the top with earth. High up the hill where the school buildings cluster, one may peer through trees and undergrowth to see a section of the wall looming over the road beneath. From the top of the school playgrounds on a clear day one may see for miles across the valley.

Much of the wall still stands on the Balkerne Hill, in some parts to a height of about thirteen feet, and just above the school only small fragments of one pedestrian way of the Balkerne Gate remains. Behind the gate, inside, is the Mercury Theatre and Jumbo the Victorian water tower. During the excavations in Balkerne Lane in 1974 the remains of four Roman wooden water pipes were discovered. This points to the possibility of a water tower in the area in Roman times. In 1552 the town records show that water was piped through the Balkerne Gate, and again in 1707, two reservoirs were placed inside the gate. Therefore Jumbo is a reminder of much that has gone before, and the school grounds lie saturated in Roman history.

At the bottom of Balkerne Hill the wall turns at right angles towards the east. At a point between St Peter's Street and Northgate Street, just above the traffic lights, a section of town wall remains sandwiched in between two shops. An excavation in 1944 on North Hill during the process of fitting a fuse box, proved the existence of a Roman North Gate, but nothing now remains.

Colchester in the south east is on the busy Pye Road from London via Chelmsford to Caistor St Edmunds. Ipswich just off the same Roman road

All that remains of the Balkerne Gate at Colchester today is a small portion of one of the pedestrian ways.

missing it by about two miles, has none of the Roman glories that the Essex town boasts. Colchester once great, and stately still, with castle grounds and walls spreading down hill. Ipswich, only fifteen miles away, with its former rampart covered with uninteresting buildings, never so great nor so grand, but still charming in places. Geographical positioning plays an important part in the historical lives of towns and cities.

Duncan says that the Rye or River Gate was not of Roman origin, but its location was determined, in Saxon or Norman times, by the necessity of providing a fall of water for milling purposes, above the ford which crossed the river, from the Roman river-gate towards the north.

Duncan's Gate or North East Gate, was named after its discoverer, Dr P. M. Duncan, when he excavated its ruins in 1853. It was small and had a single passageway ten feet high and eight feet wide, with rounded corners. It early fell into decay and disuse and was twice burnt, the second time being finally destroyed.

This, like the Balkerne Gate, was at one time blocked in with a brick wall, but archaeologists suggest it was opened again in the fourth century for passage. Dr Duncan says of his excavation, "Mingled with them (the remains of the 'arch') were human bones, horse bones, much charred wood . . . large pieces of burned fatty matter, in contact with charred wood, of disagreeable import; there were the remains of weapons, large human bones and lumps of semi-vitrified substance." The gate was probably demolished in Norman times. Today at Duncan's Gate there is green iron paling, wire netting and shrubbery, killing all opportunity to see properly the historic ruin, or absorb any of its former atmosphere.

At an early period Colchester was surrounded, or partly so, by a Town Ditch and the known sections of this ditch are marked on maps, at Scheregate, Balkerne Gate and from the tower between Rye and Duncan's Gate turning the north east corner of the town wall, to finish half-way between that corner and the East Gate.

Directly in the north east corner, inside the walls, is the Quaker cemetery, which was at one time a botanical garden, said to be comparable with Kew Gardens. Splendid trees still fill and shape the space in this quiet cemetery. In the 1860s there was a pleasure garden here, where the populace watched a balloon ascent. People also sat in the gardens which were on high ground, to watch the distant trains, then a novelty, go by.

In the back garden of the house beside the cemetery there are several steps which lead up to the embankment on the inside of the wall. During the Second World War this was a gun emplacement.

Outside the wall here, on the north east corner behind Roman Road, it is possible to see where the Town Ditch once lay. Between the wall and the new housing estate is a wide expanse of grass, planted with new trees. Here one small tree grows better, faster and stronger than the other, because it is planted inside an oval of grass, which is greener than the surrounding grass. Within this oval there was once a pond and the water still leaks through to the surface, soaking both grass and tree. This is in the dip where the large expanse of the Town Ditch formerly spread itself, and one can imagine that it may have been filled with water.

Someone who has lived in a house on the east wall all her life, told me a charming story. "When I was a little girl my brother and I used to hang over the wall, on a Sunday morning, with bread on the end of pieces of string to feed the farmer's hens low down on the outside of the wall. The hens used to jump up from below. This was our regular Sunday morning occupation. One Sunday I caught a hen! My brother and I hauled it up over the wall to release it from the constricting bread and string lodged in its throat. The hen hurried away gulping and coughing." Her mother made her confess to the farmer.

And from the same source a second story of some small boys who once attended the Gilberd School. "The small boys used to dig in the garden at the side and bottom, by the ancient wall, with their small trowels. Dig, that is for Roman treasure, and often found pieces of pottery. One day a small boy came pounding urgently on the Head's door. It might be thought that he had found a hoard of Roman coins, but on being told to 'Enter,' a furious red-faced boy said indignantly, 'Please sir, there's a second year boy in my hole.'"

We have found East Anglia to be a network of rivers and remains of ancient trackways and old Roman roads. Yearly even more of the ancient is lost underneath the webbing of new dual-carriage-ways, flyovers, and junctions. We are being opened-up by these new gashes across the landscape, which by their very nature are closing-down much of the old East Anglian world. Nevertheless I hope this book will help us to remember the past joys and sorrows of the walls. The walls of East Anglia were built by men and women great and small, known and unknown. These walls *are* the people and the people *are* the walls. They are complementary, neither could have existed without the other.

Glossary

arblaster catapult fitted with a contrivance like a powerful bow.

ashlar square freestone blocks.

bailey court or ward formed by spaces between the circuits of defences.

ballista large catapult for hurling stones.

barbican defensive enclosure in front of a gateway giving added protection.

bark, barque three or four masted sailing ship, with the fore- and main square rigged and mizzen fore-and-aft rigged.

bastion a projecting part of a fortification, either in the form of a round half tower built into the surface of the main wall, or constructed so as to form a salient angle with two faces.

belfrois high wooden tower.

bretask, bretch, bretesque, bretchia battlement or rampart.

bulwark rampart or earthwork.

bumbard primitive cannon.

burh, burg, burh, borough implies impregnable, a strong place.

burgesses inhabitants of a town.

cattus portable "room" under which soldiers could hide to move close to a defensive wall. Also known as a tortoise.

caunsey, causey, causeway way made by being trodden.

charnel (house) vault where dead bodies or bones are stored.

course even layer of stones or bricks.

coverlet counterpane.

crayls, crakys bars of iron bound together with hoops, their mouths larger than their chambers.

crenellations openings in the upper part of parapets.

culverin, culvering long, slender cannon for long range firing, first used during the sixteenth century.

curtain plain wall connecting towers or gates.

dooled dug.

ditch, whych, dych, dyke, dike hollow excavated trench for defence.

embrasure recessed opening in a rampart or fortified wall.

enciente main lines of defence of a fortified place.

espringal, springal powerful spring built into a heavy frame. Its free end held a cup-like excresence to hold the stone. Some springals also shot special heavy arrows called "garros" or quarrels.

fosse dry or wet ditch, moat or trench especially in fortifications; ditch running parallel with rampart made of materials dug from it.

garderobe toilet.

garter curtain ties.

gogeons, gudgeon, gorgions pin used in an espringal.

hackebushe earliest form of handgun—slung from a hook.

jarl man of noble birth, earl.

jebbet gallows.

justing, joust to joust, to tilt, encounter between two armed and mounted knights at a tournament.

Lollards said to take the name from Walter Lollard, founder of a sect of fanatical heretics who existed in England in the fourteenth and fifteenth centuries.

loophole   slit in a wall for light and air and to fire through.

machiolation   opening in the parapet or vault of a gateway used for projecting missiles.

marque   licence given to private persons to fit out and use ships to attack the enemy.

merlon   solid part of a battlemented wall or parapet between two openings or embrasures.

mound, maund   artifically raised heap of earth, stones, etc. raised for defensive purposes.

motte   conical mound with flat top, surrounded by a ditch.

multivallate   defence with many walls or ramparts.

murage   ancient tax levied on citizens for the building and upkeep of city walls and fortifications.

ordnance   artillery, cannon or big guns of all sizes as distinguished from small arms.

palisade   to fence with pales.

portcullis   strong, heavy, iron or timber grating, sliding up and down in grooves to open or close a castle or fortified place.

postern   a back door or gate, especially a concealed gate or exit from city walls, a castle or fort; sally — port.

procurator   an official in charge of the treasury.

quoining, quoyn   wedge shaped bricks or stones used as an angle or corner stone.

ragstone   hard bluish limestone which splits into flat masses.

rampart   mound or embankment of earth thrown up from the ditch as a defensive wall, with a broad flat top behind a stone or earthen parapet, protection, defence of any kind.

ravelin   triangular detached work placed in front of a curtain wall, placed between two bastions, on the far side of a ditch, to drive an enfilading fire across the bastions.

redan   field-work of two parapets forming a salient angle to the front with the rear open at back, joined with other defensive works.

redoubt   independent, enclosed outwork, used as a strong point in a chain of defensive works.

revetment   layer of stone or other material covering the slope of a mound or embankment to give greater strength and support.

rib   long, narrow curved section of the stonework supports on arch or vault.

rod   measure of length — five and a half yards.

sacre, saker   small sixteenth or seventeenth century cannon.

sarpetres   brass cannon firing rocks and stones.

septaria   London clay, a very poor stone.

serpentine   old form of cannon.

serf   slave working the land.

tester   canopy for bed supported on posts.

toll   tax or duty paid for the right to pass along a road, bridge or river.

tortoise   see cattus.

vallum u all um   stockade, defence of stakes, a palisaded earthworks.

villeins   feudal serfs.

wall work   the walk along the top of a town wall.

Bibliography

Addyman, P. V. and Biddle, M. Procs. Camb. Antiq. Soc. LVIII, 74-137.

Alexander, J. *Castle Hill, Cambridge.*

Alexander, J. *The Mount Pleasant Excavations and the Roman Tower Defenses.*

Andrews, I. *Boddica's Revolt*, 1972.

Astley, H. J. D. *Handbook to ancient remains of Britain and Rome at Norwich and Castle Acre*, 1913.

Atkinson, T. D. *On a Survey of the King's Ditch at Cambridge, made in 1629.*

Barker, H. R. *History of Bury St. Edmunds.*

Bayen, A. D. *A comprehensive history of Norwich, including a survey of the city.* Norwich, 1869.

Bellow, George, Sir, K.C.V.O. *Britain's Kings and Queens.*

Biddell, G. *Tilbury Fort.*

Blomefield, F. *History of the Ancient City and Burgh of Thetford, in the County of Norfolk and Suffolk*, Fersfield 1739.

Blomefield, F. *History of Norwich*, 1741.

Carter, E. *History of the County of Cambridge*, 1819.

Carter, J. I. *A Guide to Dunwich.*

Carter, J. I. and Bacon, S. R. *Ancient Dunwich*, 1975.

Charles, B. J. *People of Medieval Norwich.*

Clarke, D. T. D. *The Story of Roman Colchester*, 1967.

Clarke, D. T. D. *The Beginnings of Roman Colchester*, 1961.

Clarke, J. and D. *Camulodunum*, 1971.

Clarke, W. G. *Thetford Castle Hill*, 1907.

Claro, F. Z. *The Thames Defences.*

Clover, R. D. *Dim Corridors*, 1948.

Cunliffe, B. *Iron Age Communities in Britain*, 1975.

Collins, A. E. *The Walls of Norwich*, 1910.

Cooper, E. R. *Memories of Bygone Dunwich*, 1975.

Crummy, P. *Colchester, Recent Excavations and Research*, 1974.

Dames, M. *The Silbury Treasure.*

Darroch, E. and Taylor, B. *A Bibliography of Norfolk History*, 1975.

Dugdale, William, Sir. *The Monasticon*, Vol. IV, 1655.

Duncan, P. M., Dr. *The History and Description of the Walls of Colchester.*

Ecclestone, A. W. and J. L. *The Rise of Great Yarmouth.*

Ellison, J. A. *Excavations at Caister-on-Sea*, 1961/2.

Essex County Council. *Essex and the Sea*, 1970.

Fiennes, C. *Through England on a side saddle in the time of William and Mary*, 1695/97.

Fisher, T. *Collections — Historical, Genealogical and Topographical for Bedfordshire*, 1812-36.

Fitch, R., F.S.A., F.G.S. *An Account of Caistor Camp, near Norwich, and of antiquities found there.* Norwich, 1868.

Fitch, R., F.S.A., F.G.S. *Views of the Gates of Norwich*, 1861.

Gardner, J., Rev. *Dunwich*, 1730.

Gifford, P. R. (ed). *Cambridgeshire*, 1961.

Grandison, A. *Chronicles of Bury St. Edmunds*, 1965.

Green, B. and other. *The Parish church of Caistor St. Edmund, At Norwich, Norfolk, with a note on the Roman town.*

Green, H. J. M. *Roman Godmanchester*, Proc. Camb. Antiq. Soc. Vol. LIV. 1961.

Green, R. *History, Topography and Antiquities of Framlingham and Saxted*, 1834.

Gurney, H. *Notices of the Roman Camp at Caister and the Venta Icenorum.*

Harrod, H., F.S.A. *Castles and Convents of Norfolk*, 1857.

Harrod, H., F.S.A. *Gleaning among the Castles and Convents of Norfolk.*

Harrod, H., F.S.A. *Report on Records of Colchester*, 1865.

Harwich, The Society. *A Walk around Old Harwich*, 1973.

BIBLIOGRAPHY

Harwich, The Society. *Harwich Redoubt.*

Hawkes, J. *A Guide to the Prehistoric and Roman Monuments in England and Wales,* 1973.

Henderson, E. *The Story of Norwich.*

Hillen, J. *History of the Borough of King's Lynn,* 1917.

Houghton, B. *Saint Edmund, King and Martyr,* 1970.

Hudson, W. Rev., M.A., F.S.A. *How the City of Norwich Grew into Shape,* 1869.

Hudson. W. Rev., M.A., F.S.A. and Tingey, J. C., M.A., F.S.A. *The Records of the city of Norwich.* 1910.

Ingleby, H. *Treasures of the Lynn.* 1924.

Jewson. C. B. *People of Medieval Norwich.*

Kirkpatrick, J. *A Walk Round Norwich Walls,* 1720.

Kirkpatrick, J. *Streets and Lanes of Norwich.*

Knights, M. *The Highways and Byeways of Old Norwich,* 1887.

Loder, R. *History of Framlingham,* 1798.

Mackesy, P. J. *The Southwold Guns,* 1965 (2nd edition)

Macklin, H. W. *Bedfordshire and Huntingdonshire,* 1917.

Mallory, K. and Ohar, A. *Architecture of Aggression,* 1973.

Manship, H. *History of Great Yarmouth,* 1619.

Martin, T. *History of the Town of Thetford in the Counties of Norfolk and Suffolk, from the earliest account to the present time,* 1779.

Morant, P. *History and Antiquities of the County of Essex,* 1836.

Morris, C. Ed. *The Journeys of Celia Fiennes,* 1947.

Ninham, H. *Ancient Gates of Norwich.*

Palmer, C. J., F.S.A. *The Perlustration of Great Yarmouth,* 1872.

Pugh, R. B. (Gen. Ed). *Victoria County Histories.*

Quinton, J. (comp). *Bibliotheca Norfolciensis,* 1896.

Raby, F. J. E. *Framlingham Castle,* 1959.

Rahtz, P. A. *Pleshey Castle, a First Interim Report,* 1960.

Renn, D. and Baker, J. *Norman Castles in Britain.*

Rivet, A. L. F. *Town and Country in Roman Britain,* 1975.

Rodwell, W. and Rowley, T. *Small Towns of Roman Britain,* 1964.

Ross, A. *A Celtic intaglio from Caistor St. Edmund,* 1969.

Rye, W. *A History of Norfolk,* 1885.

Rye, W. *Catalogue of Topographical and Antiquarian Portions of the Free Library of Norwich,* 1908.

Saunders, A. D., F.M.A., F.S.A. *Tilbury Fort, Essex,* 1960.

Sitwell, C. R. *Framlingham Guide,* 1974.

Smith, J. *Essex and the Sea.*

Smith, M. L. *Early History of Witham,* 1970.

Smith, T. P. *The Medieval Defences of King's Lynn,* 1970.

Speed, J. *The Theatre of the Empire of Great Britain,* 1611.

Stark, J. *Scenery of the Rivers of Norfolk,* 1834.

Stubbs, P. *County History of England.*

Swinden, H. *History of the Antiquities of Great Yarmouth,* 1772.

Teasdell, R. H. *Great Yarmouth Town Walls.*

Tymms, S. *Bury Wills and Inventories,* 1801.

West, S. E. and Charman, D. Procs. Suffolk Institute of Archaeology. XXIX.

Whittingham, A. B., M.A., A.R.I.B.A. *Bury St. Edmunds,* 1971.

Woderspoon, J. *Memories of Ipswich,* 1850.

Wood, A., M.A., F.R.I.S.A., M.T.P.I. *Norwich City Walls,* 1970.

Wood, E. S. *Collins Field Guide to Archaeology in Britain.*

Yates, R. *History and Antiquities of the Abbey of St. Edmunds Bury* 1843.

Index

INDEX

INDEX

RS